Teach Yourself VISUALLY™

OS X El Capitan™

Paul McFedries

Visual

A Wiley Brand

Teach Yourself VISUALLY™ OS X El Capitan™

Published by
John Wiley & Sons, Inc.
10475 Crosspoint Boulevard
Indianapolis, IN 46256

www.wiley.com

Published simultaneously in Canada

Wiley publishes in a variety of print and electronic formats and by print-on-demand. Some material included with standard print versions of this book may not be included in e-books or in print-on-demand. If this book refers to media such as a CD or DVD that is not included in the version you purchased, you may download this material at http://booksupport.wiley.com. For more information about Wiley products, visit www.wiley.com.

Library of Congress Control Number: 2015951124

ISBN: 978-1-119-17387-8 (pbk); ISBN: 978-1-119-17429-5 (ebk); ISBN: 978-1-119-17391-5 (ebk)

Manufactured in the United States of America

10 9 8 7 6 5 4 3 2 1

Trademark Acknowledgments

Wiley, Visual, the Visual logo, Teach Yourself VISUALLY, Read Less - Learn More, and related trade dress are trademarks or registered trademarks of John Wiley & Sons, Inc., and/or its affiliates. OS X El Capitan is a trademark of Apple, Inc. All other trademarks are the property of their respective owners. John Wiley & Sons, Inc., is not associated with any product or vendor mentioned in this book. *Teach Yourself VISUALLY™ OS X El Capitan™* is an independent publication and has not been authorized, sponsored, or otherwise approved by Apple, Inc.

Contact Us

For general information on our other products and services, please contact our Customer Care Department within the U.S. at 877-762-2974, outside the U.S. at 317-572-3993, or fax 317-572-4002.

For technical support please visit www.wiley.com/techsupport.

Sales | Contact Wiley at (877) 762-2974 or fax (317) 572-4002.

Credits

Acquisitions Editor
Aaron Black

Project Editor
Sarah Hellert

Technical Editor
Galen Gruman

Copy Editor
Scott Tullis

Production Editor
Barath Kumar Rajasekaran

**Manager, Content Development &
Assembly**
Mary Beth Wakefield

**Vice President, Professional
Technology Strategy**
Barry Pruett

About the Author

Paul McFedries is a full-time technical writer. Paul has been authoring computer books since 1991 and he has more than 85 books to his credit. Paul's books have sold more than four million copies worldwide. These books include the Wiley titles *Teach Yourself VISUALLY OS X Yosemite*, *The Facebook Guide for People Over 50*, *iPhone Portable Genius*, 3rd Edition, and *iPad Portable Genius*, 3rd Edition. Paul is also the proprietor of Word Spy (www.wordspy.com), a website that tracks new words and phrases as they enter the language. Paul invites you to drop by his personal website at www.mcfedries.com or follow him on Twitter @wordspy.

Author's Acknowledgments

It goes without saying that writers focus on text, and I certainly enjoyed focusing on the text that you'll read in this book. However, this book is more than just the usual collection of words and phrases. A quick thumb through the pages will show you that this book is also chock-full of images, from sharp screen shots to fun and informative illustrations. Those colorful images sure make for a beautiful book, and that beauty comes from a lot of hard work by Wiley's immensely talented group of designers and layout artists. I thank them for creating another gem. Of course, what you read in this book must also be accurate, logically presented, and free of errors. Ensuring all of this was an excellent group of editors that included project editor Sarah Hellert, copy editor Scott Tullis, and technical editor Galen Gruman. Thanks to all of you for your exceptional competence and hard work. Thanks, as well, to Wiley acquisitions editor Aaron Black for asking me to write this book.

How to Use This Book

Who This Book Is For

This book is for the reader who has never used this particular technology or software application. It is also for readers who want to expand their knowledge.

The Conventions in This Book

① Steps

This book uses a step-by-step format to guide you easily through each task. Numbered steps are actions you must do; bulleted steps clarify a point, step, or optional feature; and indented steps give you the result.

② Notes

Notes give additional information — special conditions that may occur during an operation, a situation that you want to avoid, or a cross reference to a related area of the book.

③ Icons and Buttons

Icons and buttons show you exactly what you need to click to perform a step.

④ Tips

Tips offer additional information, including warnings and shortcuts.

⑤ Bold

Bold type shows command names, options, and text or numbers you must type.

⑥ Italics

Italic type introduces and defines a new term.

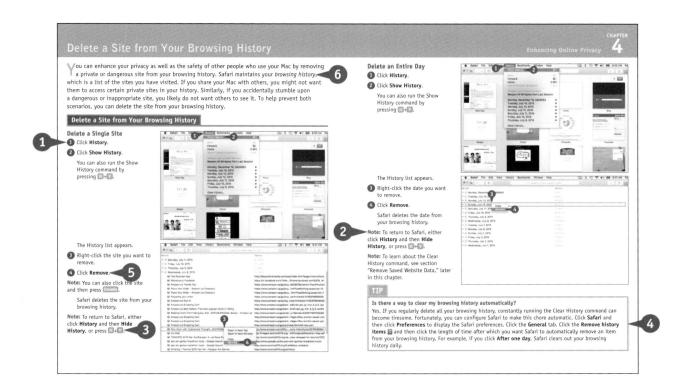

Table of Contents

Chapter 1   Learning Basic OS X Tasks

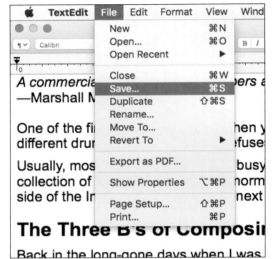

Chapter 2   Browsing the Web

Chapter 3   Communicating via Email

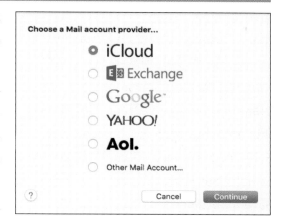

Chapter 4   Enhancing Online Privacy

Table of Contents

Chapter 5   Talking via Messages and FaceTime

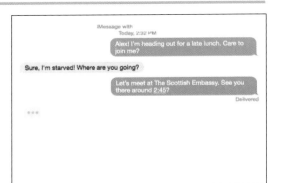

Chapter 6   Tracking Contacts and Events

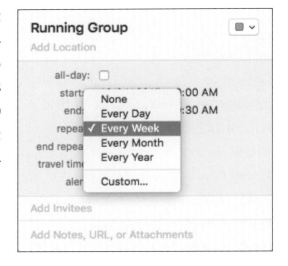

Chapter 7 — Playing and Organizing Music

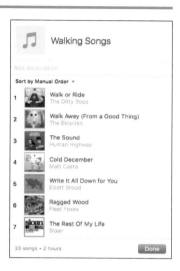

Chapter 8 — Learning Useful OS X Tasks

Table of Contents

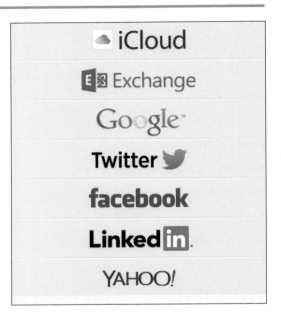

Chapter 11   Securing OS X

Chapter 12   Customizing OS X

Table of Contents

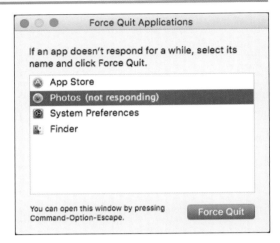

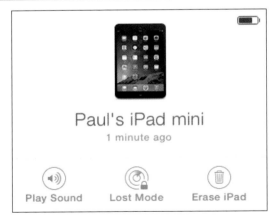

Chapter 15 Networking with OS X

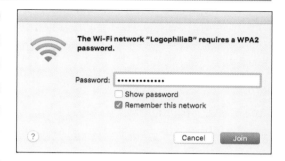

CHAPTER 1

Learning Basic OS X Tasks

OS X has a few basic tasks that you need to know to make the rest of Mac chores faster and easier. These chores include starting and managing applications, searching your Mac for documents and data, saving your work, and fundamental file operations such as opening, printing, and copying.

Start an Application

To perform tasks of any kind in OS X, you use one of the applications installed on your Mac. The application you use depends on the task you want to perform. For example, if you want to surf the World Wide Web, you use a web browser application, such as the Safari program that comes with OS X. Before you can use an application, however, you must first tell OS X what application you want to run. OS X launches the application and displays it on the desktop. You can then use the application's tools to perform your tasks.

Start an Application

Using the Dock

1 If the application that you want to start has an icon in the Dock, click the icon to start the application.

A Move the mouse (🖰) over a Dock icon to see the name of the application.

Using Spotlight

1 Click **Spotlight** (🔍).

2 Start typing the name of the application you want to start.

B OS X displays a list of matching items.

3 When the application appears in the results, click it to start the program.

4

Using Finder

1 Click **Finder** ( ).

The Finder window appears.

2 Click **Applications**.

Note: You can also open Applications in any Finder window by pressing **Shift**+**⌘**+**A** or by clicking **Go** and then clicking **Applications**.

3 Double-click the application you want to start.

Note: In some cases, double-clicking the icon just displays the contents of a folder. In this case, you then double-click the application icon.

C The application appears on the desktop.

D OS X adds a button for the application to the Dock.

E The menu bar displays the menus associated with the application.

Note: Another common way to launch an application is to use Finder to locate a document you want to work with and then double-click that document.

TIPS

How do I add an icon to the Dock for an application I use frequently?

To add an icon to the Dock, repeat steps **1** to **3** in the subsection "Using Finder." Right-click the application's Dock icon, click **Options**, and then click **Keep in Dock**.

How do I shut down a running application?

To shut down a running application, right-click the application's Dock icon and then click **Quit**. Alternatively, you can switch to the application and press **⌘**+**Q**.

Start an Application Using Launchpad

You can start an application using the Launchpad feature. This is often faster than using the Applications folder, particularly for applications that do not have a Dock icon.

Launchpad is designed to mimic the Home screens of the iPhone, iPad, and iPod touch. So if you own one or more of these devices, then you are already familiar with how Launchpad works.

Start an Application Using Launchpad

① Click **Launchpad** ( ).

The Launchpad screen appears.

② If the application you want to start resides in a different Launchpad screen, click the dot that corresponds to the screen.

Launchpad switches to the screen and displays the applications.

③ If the application you want to start resides within a folder, click the folder.

Launchpad opens the folder.

④ Click the icon of the application you want to start.

Note: To exit Launchpad without starting an application, press Esc.

OS X starts the application.

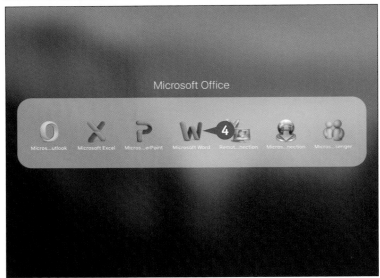

Locate the Mouse Pointer

OS X El Capitan includes a new feature that helps you locate the mouse pointer. This is useful because although you can control certain features of OS X using the keyboard or by using gestures on a trackpad or similar device, most OS X tasks require the mouse. Clicking, double-clicking, dragging, and other standard mouse techniques make using OS X easy and efficient, but not if you have trouble locating the mouse pointer. This can happen very easily if your screen is crowded with windows.

Locate the Mouse Pointer

1 Jiggle the pointer several times:

If you have a mouse, move the mouse back and forth.

If you have a trackpad or a Magic Mouse, slide your finger back and forth on the surface of the trackpad or the top of the Magic Mouse.

A OS X temporarily increases the size of the mouse (**k**).

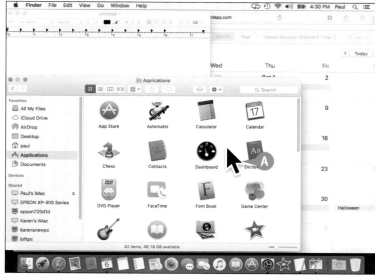

Switch Between Applications

If you plan on running multiple applications at the same time, you need to know how to easily switch from one application to another. In OS X, after you start one application, you do not need to close that application before you open another one. OS X supports a feature called *multitasking*, which means running two or more applications simultaneously. This is handy if you need to use several applications throughout the day.

Switch Between Applications

1 Click the Dock icon of the application you want to switch to.

Note: If you can see part of the application's window, you can also switch to the application by clicking its window.

A OS X brings the application window(s) to the foreground.

B The menu bar displays the menus associated with the application.

Note: To switch between applications from the keyboard, press and hold ⌘ and repeatedly press **Tab** until the application that you want is highlighted in the list of running applications. Release ⌘ to switch to the application.

View Running Applications with Mission Control

The Mission Control feature makes it easier for you to navigate and locate your running applications. OS X allows you to open multiple applications simultaneously, and the only real limit to the number of open applications you can have is the amount of memory contained in your Mac. In practical terms, this means you can easily open several applications, some of which may have multiple open windows. To help locate and navigate to the window you need, use the Mission Control feature.

View Running Applications with Mission Control

1 Click **Launchpad** (![icon]).

2 Click **Mission Control**.

Note: You can also invoke Mission Control by pressing F3 or by placing four fingers on the trackpad of your Mac and then swiping up.

A Mission Control displays each open window.

To switch to a particular window, click it.

B To close Mission Control without selecting a window, click **Desktop** or press Esc.

Run an Application Full Screen

You can maximize the viewing and working areas of an application by running that application in full-screen mode. When you switch to full-screen mode, OS X hides the menu bar, the application's status bar, the Dock, and the top section of the application window (the section that includes the Close, Minimize, and Zoom buttons). OS X then expands the rest of the application window so that it takes up the entire screen. Note that not all programs are capable of switching to full-screen mode.

Run an Application Full Screen

1 Click **View**.

2 Click **Enter Full Screen**.

You can also press Control + ⌘ + F.

A In applications that support Full Screen, you can also click **Zoom** (●).

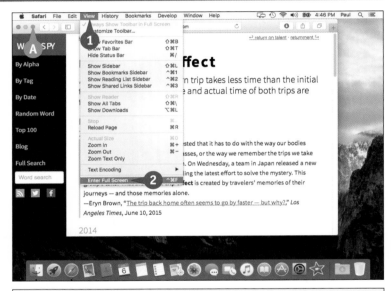

3 OS X expands the application window to take up the entire screen.

Note: To exit full-screen mode, move the mouse (↖) up to the top of the screen to reveal the menu bar, click **View**, and then click **Exit Full Screen**. You can also click **Zoom** (●), press Esc, or Control + ⌘ + F.

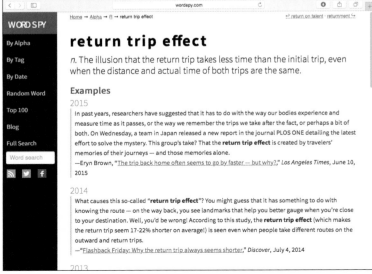

Split the Screen with Two Applications

You can make your OS X desktop more convenient and more efficient by splitting the screen with two application windows. Splitting the screen means that one application window takes up the left side of the desktop, and a second application window takes up the right side of the desktop. With these windows arranged side by side, the content of both windows remains visible at all times, so you can easily refer to one window while working in the other.

Split the Screen with Two Applications

1 Click and hold **Zoom** (⬤).

2 Drag the mouse (⬈) to either the left or the right side of the screen.

A OS X displays a blue background to show you where the application window will reside.

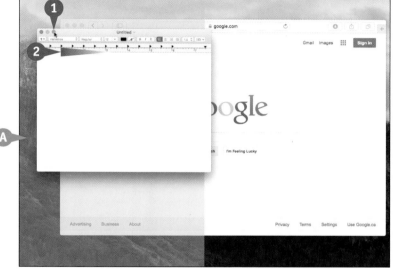

3 Release the mouse.

B OS X switches to full-screen mode and displays the application in the half of the screen you selected.

C OS X displays thumbnail versions of the other open windows.

4 Click a window.

OS X displays the window in the other half of the screen.

Note: To exit split-screen mode, move the mouse (⬈) to the top of the screen, click **View**, and then click **Exit Full Screen**. You can also click **Zoom** (⬤), press Esc, or Control + ⌘ + F.

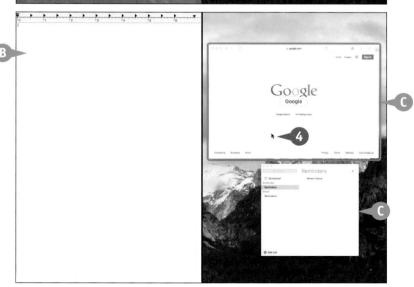

Search Your Mac

You can save time and make your Mac easier to use by learning how to search for the apps, settings, or files that you need.

After you have used your Mac for a while and have created many documents, you might have trouble locating a specific file. You can save a great deal of time by using OS X's Spotlight search feature to search for your document. You can also use Spotlight to search for apps as well as information from the Internet, the iTunes Store, the App Store, and more. Alternatively, you can use Finder's Search box to search just your Mac.

Search Your Mac

Search with Spotlight

1 Click **Spotlight** (🔍).

You can also press ⌘+**Spacebar**.

A The Spotlight window appears.

2 Type a word or short phrase that represents the item or information you want to locate.

B As you type, Spotlight displays the Mac and online items that match your search text.

3 Click the item you want to view or work with.

OS X opens the item.

Search Your Mac

1 Click **Finder** ( ).

2 If you want to search within a specific folder, open that folder.

3 Click inside the Search box.

4 Type a word or short phrase that represents the item you want to locate.

C As you type, Spotlight displays the items that match your search text.

D If you are searching a specific folder, you can click **This Mac** to switch to searching your entire Mac.

5 Click the item you want to work with.

OS X opens the item.

TIP

Can I remove item types from the Spotlight search results?

Yes. Spotlight supports a number of different *categories*, such as Applications, Documents, and Contacts. If there are categories that you never search for, such as system preferences or movies, you should remove them to make it easier to navigate the Spotlight search results.

To remove one or more categories from the Spotlight results, click **System Preferences** ( ) in the Dock and then click **Spotlight**. In the Search Results pane, click the check box beside each category you want to remove (changes to).

Save a Document

After you create a document and make changes to it, you can save the document to preserve your work. When you work on a document, OS X stores the changes in your computer's memory. However, OS X erases the contents of the Mac's memory each time you shut down or restart the computer. This means that the changes you make to your document are lost when you turn off or restart your Mac. However, saving the document preserves your changes on your Mac's hard drive.

Save a Document

1 Click **File**.

2 Click **Save**.

In most applications, you can also press ⌘+S.

If you have saved the document previously, your changes are now preserved, and you do not need to follow the rest of the steps in this section.

If this is a new document that you have never saved before, the Save As dialog appears.

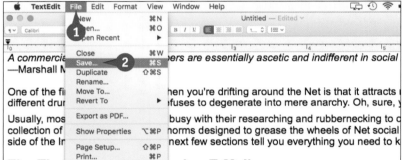

3 Type the filename you want to use in the Save As text box.

Ⓐ To store the file in a different folder, you can click the **Where** ⬍ and then select the location that you prefer from the pop-up menu.

4 Click **Save**.

The application saves the file.

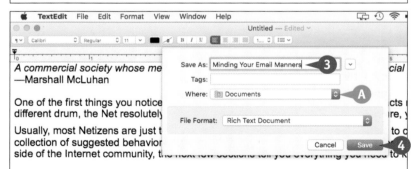

Open a Document

To work with a document that you have saved in the past, you can open it in the application that you used to create it. When you save a document, you save its contents to your Mac's hard drive, and those contents are stored in a separate file. When you open the document using the same application that you used to save it, OS X loads the file's contents into memory and displays the document in the application. You can then view or edit the document as needed.

Open a Document

1 Start the application you want to work with.

2 Click **File**.

3 Click **Open**.

In most applications, you can also press ⌘+O.

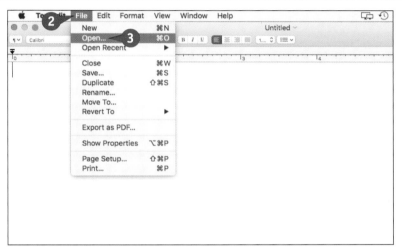

The Open dialog appears.

A To select a different folder from which to open a file, you can click ⟨ and then click the location that you prefer.

4 Click the document.

5 Click **Open**.

The document appears in a window on the desktop.

Print a Document

When you need a hard copy of your document, either for your files or to distribute to someone else, you can send the document to your printer. Most applications that deal with documents also come with a Print command. When you run this command, the Print dialog appears. You use the Print dialog to choose the printer you want, as well as to specify how many copies you want to print. Many Print dialogs also enable you to see a preview of your document before printing it.

Print a Document

1 Turn on your printer.

2 Open the document that you want to print.

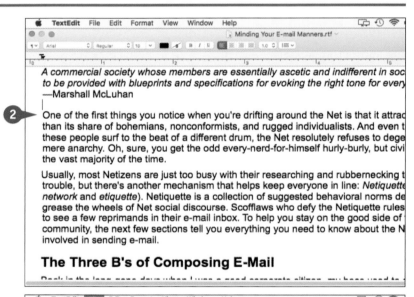

3 Click **File**.

4 Click **Print**.

In many applications, you can select the Print command by pressing ⌘+P.

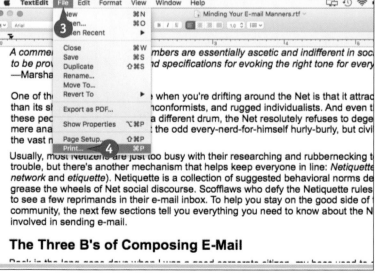

The Print dialog appears.

The layout of the Print dialog varies from application to application. The version shown here is a typical example.

⑤ If you have more than one printer, click the **Printer** 🔾 to select the printer that you want to use.

⑥ To print more than one copy, type the number of copies to print in the Copies text box.

⑦ Click **Print**.

Ⓐ OS X prints the document. The printer's icon appears in the Dock while the document prints.

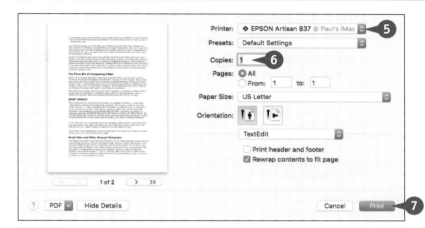

TIP

Can I print only part of my document?

Yes, you can print either a single page or a range of pages, although the steps you use to specify what you want to print vary from one application to another. In the Pages word processing application, for example, you use the Pages pop-up menu to select what you want to print: All, Single, or Range.

If you select the Single option, use the text box (or the stepper, 🔾) to specify the number of the page you want to print.

If you select the Range option, use the two text boxes (or their associated steppers, 🔾) to specify the numbers of the first and last pages you want to print.

Copy a File

You can use OS X to make an exact copy of a file. This is useful when you want to make an extra copy of an important file to use as a backup. Similarly, you might require a copy of a file if you want to send the copy on a disk to another person. Finally, copying a file is also a real timesaver if you need a new file very similar to an existing file: You copy the original file and then make the required changes to the copy. You can copy either a single file or multiple files. You can also use this technique to copy a folder.

Copy a File

1 Locate the file that you want to copy.

2 Open the folder to which you want to copy the file.

To open a second folder window, click **File** and then click **New Finder Window**, or press ⌘+N.

3 Press and hold **Option**, and then click and drag the file and drop it inside the destination folder.

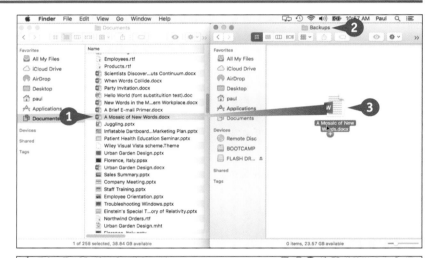

A The original file remains in its folder.

B A copy of the original file appears in the destination folder.

You can also make a copy of a file in the same folder, which is useful if you want to make major changes to the file and you would like to preserve a copy of the original. Click the file, click **File**, and then click **Duplicate**, or press ⌘+D. OS X creates a copy with the word "copy" added to the filename.

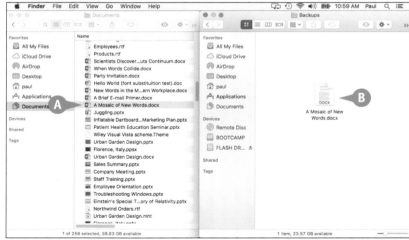

Move a File

When you need to store a file in a new location, the easiest way is to move the file from its current folder to another folder on your Mac. When you save a file for the first time, you specify a folder on your Mac's hard drive. This original location is not permanent, however. Using the technique in this section, you can move the file to another location on your Mac's hard drive. You can use this technique to move a single file, multiple files, and even a folder.

Move a File

1 Locate the file that you want to move.

2 Open the folder to which you want to move the file.

To create a new destination folder in the current folder, click **File** and then click **New Folder**, or press <kbd>Shift</kbd>+<kbd>⌘</kbd>+<kbd>N</kbd>.

3 Click and drag the file and drop it inside the destination folder.

Note: If you are moving the file to another drive, you must press and hold ⌘ while you click and drag the file. Otherwise a copy is made.

Ⓐ The file disappears from its original folder.

Ⓑ The file moves to the destination folder.

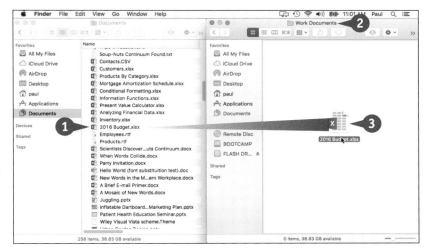

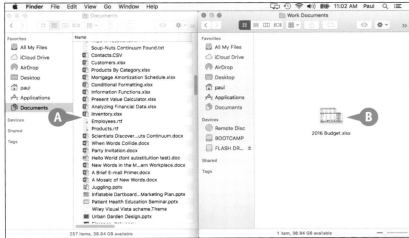

Rename a File

You can change the name of a file, which is useful if the current filename does not accurately describe the contents of the file. Giving your document a descriptive name makes it easier to find the file later. You should rename only those documents that you have created or that have been given to you by someone else. Do not try to rename any of the OS X system files or any files associated with your applications, or your computer may behave erratically or even crash.

Rename a File

1 Open the folder containing the file that you want to rename.

2 Click the file.

3 Press **Return**.

A A text box appears around the filename.

You can also rename any folders that you have created.

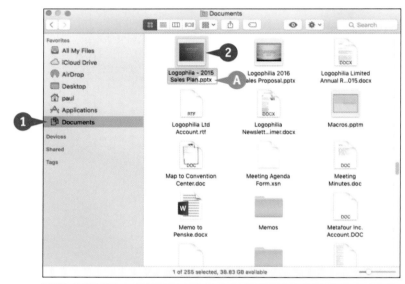

4 Edit the existing name or type a new name that you want to use for the file.

If you decide that you do not want to rename the file after all, you can press **Esc** to cancel the operation.

5 Press **Return** or click an empty section of the folder.

The new name appears under the file icon.

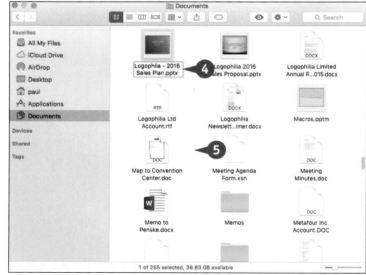

Delete a File

When you no longer need a file, you can delete it. This helps to prevent your hard drive from becoming cluttered with unnecessary files. You should ensure that you delete only those documents that you have created or that have been given to you by someone else. Do not delete any of the OS X system files or any files associated with your applications, or your computer may behave erratically or even crash.

Delete a File

1 Locate the file that you want to delete.

2 Click and drag the file and drop it on the **Trash** icon (🗑) in the Dock.

A The file disappears from the folder.

You can also delete a file by clicking it and then pressing ⌘+Delete.

If you delete a file accidentally, you can restore it. Click the Dock's **Trash** icon (🗑) to open the Trash window. Right-click the file and then click **Put Back**.

Open a Folder in a Tab

You can make it easier to work with multiple folders simultaneously by opening each folder in its own tab within a single Finder window. As you work with your documents, you may come upon one or more folders that you want to keep available while you work with other folders. Instead of cluttering the desktop with multiple Finder windows, OS X enables you to use a single Finder window that displays each open folder in a special section of the window called a *tab*. To view the contents of any open folder, you need only click its tab.

Open a Folder in a Tab

Open a Folder in a New Tab

1 Right-click the folder you want to open.

2 Click **Open in New Tab**.

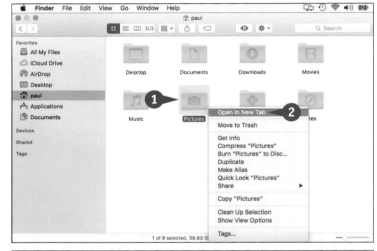

A A new tab appears for the folder.

B The folder's contents appear here.

C Click any tab to display its contents in the Finder window.

D To close a tab, position the mouse (⬆) over the tab and then click **Close Tab** (✕).

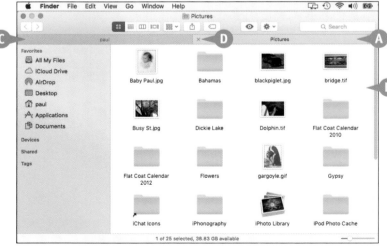

22

Create a New Tab

1 Click **File**.

2 Click **New Tab**.

E If you already have two or more tabs open, you can also click **Create a new tab** (+).

Finder creates a new tab.

Merge Open Folder Windows into Tabs

1 Click **Window**.

2 Click **Merge All Windows**.

Finder moves all the open folder windows into tabs in a single Finder window.

Note: To copy or move a file to a folder open in another tab, click and drag the file from its current folder and drop it on the other folder's tab.

TIP

Are there any shortcuts I can use to work with folders in tabs?

- In a folder, press and hold ⌘ and double-click a subfolder to open it in a tab. Press and hold ⌘+Shift instead to open the subfolder in a tab without switching to the tab.
- In the sidebar, press and hold ⌘ (or ⌘+Shift) and click a folder to open it in a tab.
- Press Shift+⌘+] or Shift+⌘+[to cycle through the tabs.
- Press ⌘+W to close the current tab.
- Press Option and click **Close Tab** (✕) to close every tab but the one you clicked.

CHAPTER 2

Browsing the Web

If your Mac is connected to the Internet, you can use the Safari browser to navigate, or *surf*, websites. Safari offers features that make it easier to browse the web. For example, you can open multiple pages in a single Safari window and you can save your favorite sites for easier access.

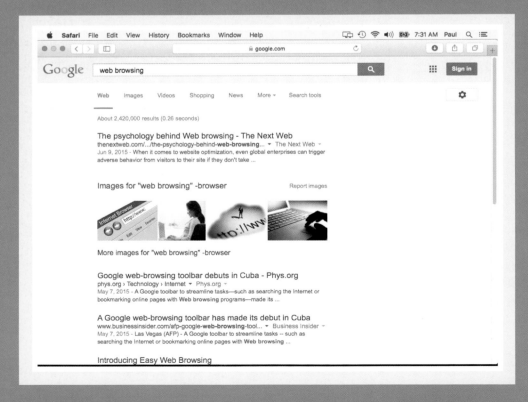

Open a Web Page in a Tab

You can make it easier to work with multiple web pages and sites simultaneously by opening each page in its own tab. As you surf the web, you may come upon a page that you want to keep available while you visit other sites. Instead of leaving the page and trying to find it again when you need it, Safari lets you leave the page open in a special section of the browser window called a *tab*. You can then use a second tab to visit your other sites, and to resume viewing the first site, you need only click its tab.

Open a Web Page in a Tab

Open a Link in a New Tab

1 Right-click the link you want to open.

2 Click **Open Link in New Tab**.

A A new tab appears with the page title.

3 Click the tab to display the page.

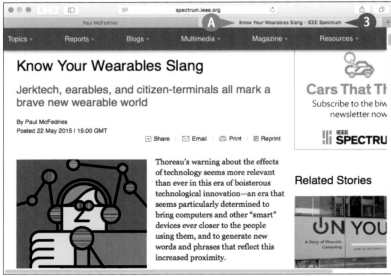

Create a New Tab

1 Click **File**.

2 Click **New Tab**.

B You can also click **Create a new tab** ($+$).

C Safari creates a new tab and displays the Top Sites tab.

After you have used Safari for a while, the Top Sites tab lists the websites that you have visited most often.

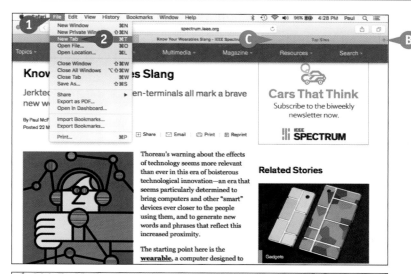

3 Type the address of the page you want to load into the new tab.

4 Press **Return**.

D Safari displays the page in the tab.

TIP

Are there any shortcuts I can use to open web pages in tabs?

Yes, here are a few useful keyboard techniques you can use:

- Press and hold ⌘ and click a link to open the page in a tab.
- Type an address and then press ⌘+**Return** to open the page in a new tab.
- Press **Shift**+⌘+**]** or **Shift**+⌘+**[** to cycle through the tabs.
- Press ⌘+**W** to close the current tab.

Navigate Web Pages

After you have visited several pages, you can return to a page you visited earlier. Instead of retyping the address or looking for the link, Safari gives you some easier methods. When you navigate from page to page, you create a kind of path through the web. Safari keeps track of this path by maintaining a list of the pages you visit. You can use that list to go back to a page you have visited. After you go back to a page you have visited, you can use the same list to go forward through the pages again.

Navigate Web Pages

Go Back One Page

1 Click **Previous Page** (<).

The previous page you visited appears.

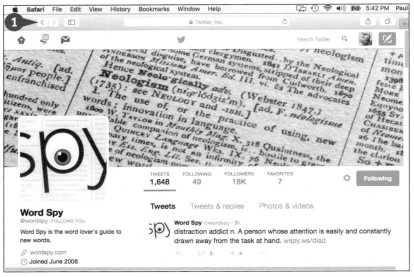

Go Back Several Pages

1 Click and hold down the mouse (▶) on **Previous Page** (<).

A list of the pages you have visited appears.

Note: The list of visited pages is different for each tab that you have open. If you do not see the page you want, you may need to click a different tab.

2 Click the page you want to revisit.

The page appears.

Go Forward One Page

1 Click **Next Page** (>).

The next page appears.

Note: If you are at the last page viewed up to that point, the Next Page icon (>) is not active.

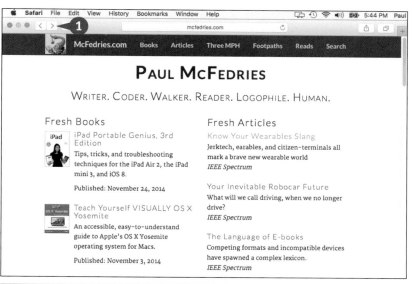

Go Forward Several Pages

1 Click and hold down the mouse (⬉) on **Next Page** (>).

A list of the pages you have visited appears.

Note: The list of visited pages is different for each tab that you have open. If you do not see the page you want, you may need to click a different tab.

2 Click the page you want to revisit.

The page appears.

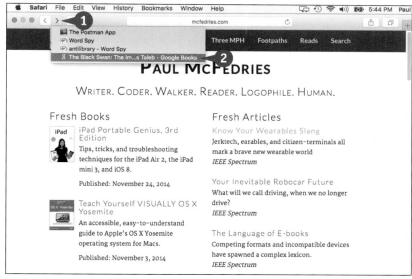

Are there any shortcuts I can use to navigate web pages?

Yes, a few useful keyboard shortcuts you can use are:

- Press ⌘+[to go back one page.
- Press ⌘+] to go forward one page.
- Press Shift+⌘+H to return to the Safari home page (the first page you see when you open Safari).

Navigate with the History List

The Previous Page and Next Page icons (< and >) enable you to navigate pages in the current browser session. To redisplay sites that you have visited in the past few days or weeks, you need to use the History list, which is a collection of the websites and pages you have visited over the past month.

If you visit sensitive places such as an Internet banking site or your corporate site, you can increase security by clearing the History list so that other people cannot see where you have been.

Navigate with the History List

Load a Page from the Recent History List

1 Click **History**.

Safari displays a menu of recent dates that you used the program.

2 Click the date when you visited the page.

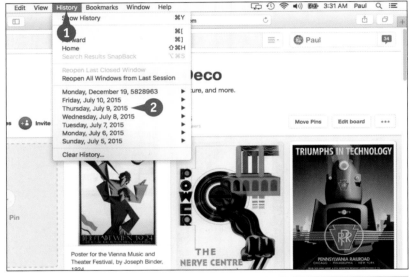

A A submenu of pages that you visited during that day appears.

3 Click the page you want to revisit.

Safari opens the page.

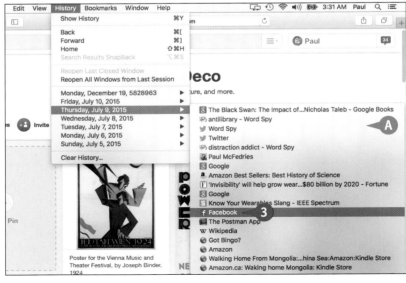

Load a Page from the Full History List

1 Click **History**.

2 Click **Show History**.

Note: You can also run the Show History command by pressing ⌘+Y.

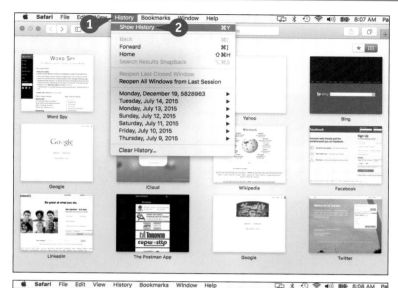

Safari displays the full History list.

3 Double-click the date when you visited the page.

B A submenu of pages that you visited during that day appears.

4 Double-click the page you want to revisit.

Safari opens the page.

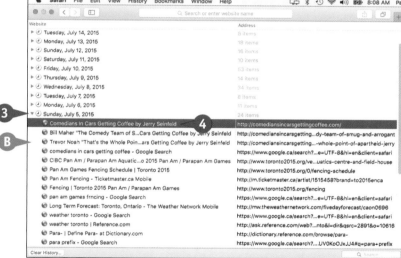

How can I control the length of time that Safari keeps track of the pages I visit?

In the menu bar, click **Safari** and then **Preferences**. The Safari preferences appear. Click the **General** tab. Click the **Remove history items** ⬦ and then select the amount of time you want Safari to track your history. Click **Close** (⬤).

Is there an easier way to find the page I am looking for?

If you know some or all of the page's title or address, you can search for the page. Press ⌘+Y to open History, click the Search box in the lower right corner, and then type what you can remember of the page title or address.

Change Your Home Page

Your home page is the web page that appears when you first start Safari. The default home page is usually the Apple.com Start page, but you can change that to any other page you want, or even to an empty page. This is useful if you do not use the Apple.com Start page, or if there is another page that you always visit at the start of your browsing session. For example, if you have your own website, it might make sense to always begin there. Safari also comes with a command that enables you to view the home page at any time during your browsing session.

Change Your Home Page

Change the Home Page

1 Display the web page that you want to use as your home page.

2 Click **Safari**.

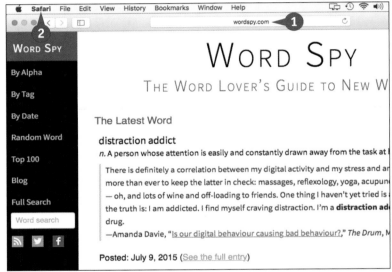

3 Click **Preferences**.

4 Click **General**.

5 Click **Set to Current Page**.

Ⓐ Safari inserts the address of the current page in the Homepage text box.

Note: If your Mac is not currently connected to the Internet, you can also type the new home page address manually using the Homepage text box.

6 Click **Close** (⬤).

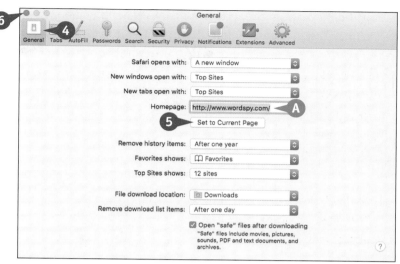

View the Home Page

1 Click **History**.

2 Click **Home**.

Note: You can also display the home page by pressing Shift + ⌘ + H.

Safari displays the home page.

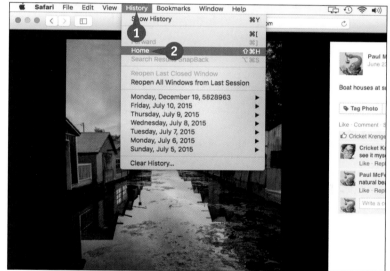

TIP

How can I get Safari to open a new tab without displaying the home page?
In the menu bar, click **Safari** and then **Preferences**. The Safari preferences appear. Click the **General** tab. Click the **New tabs open with** ⬦ and then select **Empty Page** (Ⓐ) from the pop-up menu. Click **Close** (⬤) to close the Safari preferences.

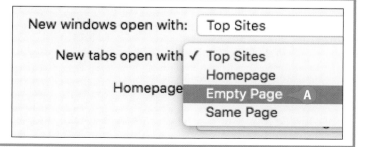

Bookmark Web Pages

If you have web pages that you visit frequently, you can save yourself time by storing those pages as bookmarks — also called favorites — within Safari. This enables you to display the pages with just a couple of mouse clicks.

The bookmark stores the name as well as the address of the page. Most bookmarks are stored on the Safari Bookmarks menu. However, Safari also offers the Favorites bar, which appears just below the address bar. You can put your favorite sites on the Favorites bar for easiest access.

Bookmark Web Pages

Bookmark a Web Page

1. Display the web page you want to save as a bookmark.

2. Click **Bookmarks**.

3. Click **Add Bookmark**.

Ⓐ You can also run the Add Bookmark command by clicking **Share** (🔼) and then clicking **Add Bookmark**.

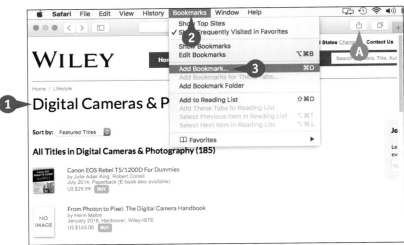

The Add Bookmark dialog appears.

Note: You can also display the Add Bookmark dialog by pressing ⌘+D.

4. Click ⬍ and then click the location where you want to store the bookmark.

5. Edit the page name, if necessary.

6. Click **Add**.

Safari adds a bookmark for the page.

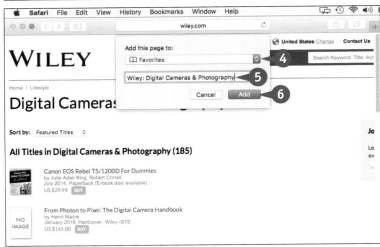

Display a Bookmarked Web Page

1 Click **Show sidebar** ().

2 Click **Bookmarks** ().

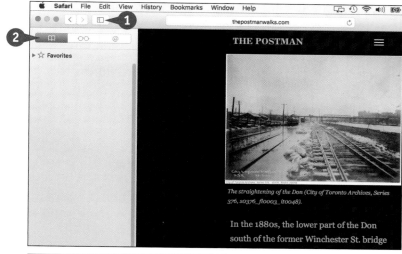

The sidebar appears with the Bookmarks tab displayed.

3 Click the location of the bookmark, such as **Favorites**.

4 Click the folder that contains the bookmark you want to display.

5 Click the bookmark.

The web page appears.

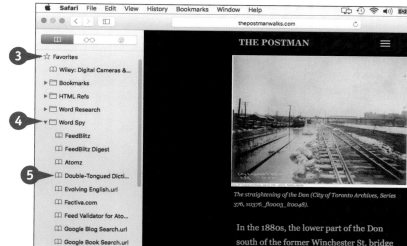

Is there an easier way to display favorite pages?

Yes. Click **View** and then click **Show Favorites Bar**. Safari assigns keyboard shortcuts to the first nine bookmarks, counting from left to right and excluding folders. Display the leftmost bookmark by pressing ⌘+1. Moving to the right, the shortcuts are ⌘+2, ⌘+3, and so on.

How do I delete a bookmark?

If the site is on the Favorites bar, right-click the bookmark and then click **Delete**, or press and hold ⌘ and drag it off the bar. For all other bookmarks, click **Show sidebar** () and then **Bookmarks** () to display the sidebar's Bookmarks tab. Locate the bookmark to remove, right-click the bookmark, and then click **Delete**.

Pin a Web Page Tab

If you have one or more web pages that you access frequently, you might want even easier access to those pages than you get when you bookmark them. For example, you might want the web page to be available every time you launch Safari and every time you open a new Safari window. You can have that convenience and efficiency by using Safari to pin a web page's tab. This places a small icon for the tab to the left of the current tabs in every open Safari window. The pinned tabs also stay in place when you close and reopen Safari.

Pin a Web Page Tab

1 Open the web page you want to pin.

2 Click **Window**.

3 Click **Pin Tab**.

A You can also pin a tab by dragging the tab to the left of the existing tabs.

B Safari pins the tab.

C To open the tab, you can either right-click the pinned tab and then click **Unpin Tab**, or drag the pinned tab to the right.

Note: To remove the pinned tab, right-click it and then click **Close Tab**.

Mute a Web Page Tab

I f a web page tab is playing sound, but you are not sure which tab is the source of the audio, you can have Safari mute all the open tabs. Having many web pages open in tabs is convenient, but a tab might suddenly begin playing sound, likely an ad or video that had a delayed start. The more tabs you have open, the less likely you are to know which tab is playing the sound. To avoid this frustration, tell Safari to mute all the tabs.

Mute a Web Page Tab

1 On the tab that is playing sound, click **Mute This Tab** (◁ᵢ)).

A If multiple tabs are playing sound, you can mute them all by switching to a tab that is not playing audio and then clicking **Mute Other Tabs** (◁ᵢ)) in the address bar.

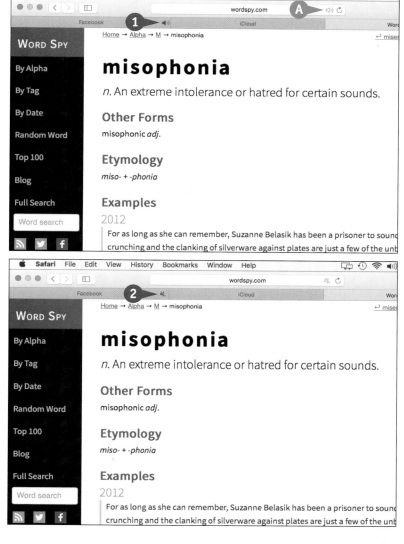

Safari mutes the sound (◁ᵢ) changes to ◁).

2 To resume playing the sound, click **Unmute This Tab** (◁).

Search for Sites

If you need information on a specific topic, Safari has a built-in feature that enables you to quickly search the web for sites that have the information you require. The web has a number of sites called *search engines* that enable you to find what you are looking for. By default, Safari uses the Google search site (www.google.com). Simple, one-word searches often return tens of thousands of *hits*, or matching sites. To improve your searching, type multiple search terms that define what you are looking for. To search for a phrase, enclose the words in quotation marks.

Search for Sites

1 Click in the address bar.

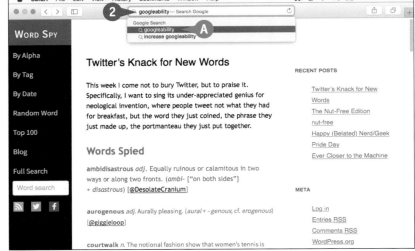

2 Type a word, phrase, or question that represents the information you want to find.

Ⓐ If you see the search text you want to use in the list of suggested searches, click the text and skip step **3**.

3 Press Return.

B A list of pages that matches your search text appears.

4 Click a web page.

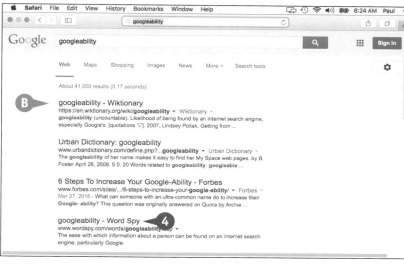

The page appears.

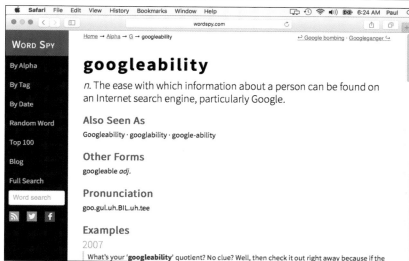

Is there an easy way that I can rerun a recent search?

Yes, you can use Safari's SnapBack feature to quickly rerun your search. In the menu bar, click **History** and then click **Search Results SnapBack** (or press Option+⌘+S). Safari sends the search text to the search again.

How do I change the search engine that Safari uses?

In the menu bar, click **Safari** and then click **Preferences** to open Safari's preferences. Click the **Search** tab, click the **Search engine** ◉, and then click the search engine you prefer: Google, Yahoo, Bing, or DuckDuckGo.

Download a File

Some websites make files available for you to open on your Mac. To use these files, you can download them to your Mac using Safari. Saving data from the Internet to your computer is called *downloading*. For certain types of files, Safari may display the content right away instead of letting you download it. This happens for files such as text documents and PDF files. In any case, to use a file from a website, you must have an application designed to work with that particular file type. For example, if the file is an Excel workbook, you need either Excel for the Mac or a compatible program.

Download a File

1 Navigate to the page that contains the link to the file.

2 Scroll down and click the link to the file.

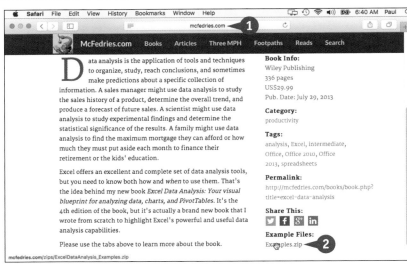

Safari downloads the file to your Mac.

Ⓐ The Show Downloads button shows the progress of the download.

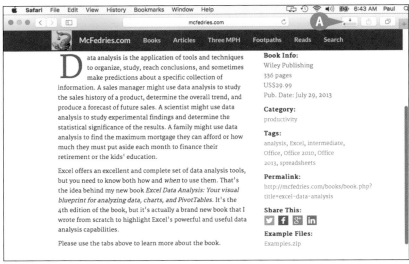

3 When the download is complete, click **Show Downloads** (⬇).

4 Right-click the file.

B You can also double-click the icon to the left of the file.

C You can click **Show in Finder** (🔍) to view the file in the Downloads folder.

5 Click **Open**.

The file opens in Finder (in the case of a compressed Zip file, as shown here) or in the corresponding application.

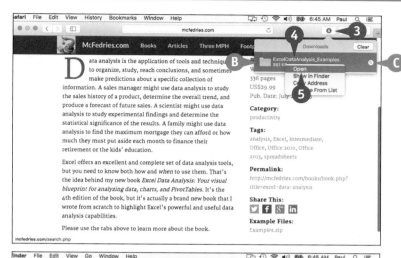

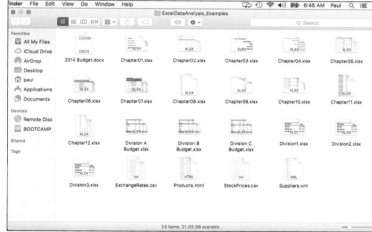

TIPS

If Safari displays the file instead of downloading it, how do I save the file to my Mac?

Click **File** and then click **Save As**. Type a name for the new file, choose a folder, and then click **Save**.

Is it safe to download files from the web?

Yes, but download files only from sites you trust. If you notice that Safari is attempting to download a file without your permission, cancel the download immediately; the file likely contains a virus or other malware. Fortunately, OS X has built-in safeguards against installing malware, so even if you download a malware program by accident, OS X will not allow it to be installed.

View Links Shared on Social Networks

You can make your web surfing more interesting and your social networking more efficient by using Safari to directly access links shared by the people you follow. Social networks are about connecting with people, but a big part of that experience is sharing information, particularly links to interesting, useful, or entertaining web pages. You normally have to log in to the social network to see these links, but if you have used OS X to sign in to your accounts, you can use Safari to directly access links shared by your Twitter and LinkedIn connections.

View Links Shared on Social Networks

Note: For more information on signing in to your social networking accounts, see Chapter 9.

1 Click **Show sidebar** (⬚).

The Bookmarks sidebar appears.

2 Click **Shared Links** (@).

Safari displays the Shared Links sidebar, which lists the most recent links shared by the people you follow on Twitter and LinkedIn.

③ Click the shared link you want to view.

Ⓐ Safari displays the linked web page.

Ⓑ For a Twitter link, if you want to retweet the link to your followers, click **Retweet**.

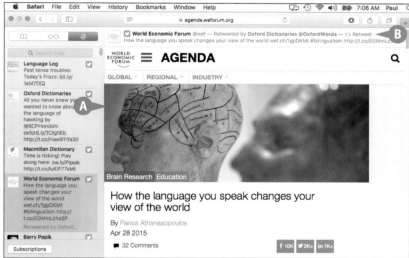

How can I be sure that I am seeing the most recent shared links?

Safari usually updates the Shared Links list each time you open it. However, to be sure that you are seeing the most recent links shared by people you follow on Twitter or are connected to on LinkedIn, click the **View** menu and then click **Update Shared Links**.

How do I hide the Shared Links sidebar when I do not need it?

To give yourself more horizontal screen area for viewing pages, hide the sidebar by clicking **Show sidebar** (⬛) again. You can also toggle the Shared Links sidebar on and off by pressing Control + ⌘ + 3.

Create a Web Page Reading List

If you do not have time to read a web page now, you can add the page to your Reading List and then read the page later when you have time. You will often come upon a page with fascinating content that you want to read, but lack the time. You could bookmark the article, but bookmarks are really for pages you want to revisit often, not for those you might read only once. A better solution is to add the page to the Reading List, which is a simple list of pages you save to read later.

Create a Web Page Reading List

Add a Page to the Reading List

1 Navigate to the page you want to read later.

2 Click **Bookmarks**.

3 Click **Add to Reading List**.

Safari adds the page to the Reading List.

Select a Page from the Reading List

1 Click **Show sidebar** (⬚).

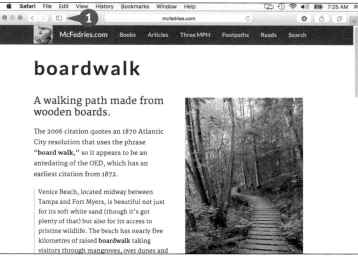

The Bookmarks sidebar appears.

2 Click **Reading List** (∞).

3 Drag the list down slightly to see the controls.

4 Click **Unread**.

Ⓐ If you want to reread a page you have read previously, click **All** instead.

5 Click the page.

Ⓑ Safari displays the page.

TIP

Are there easier ways to add a web page to my Reading List?

Yes, Safari offers several shortcut methods you can use. The easiest is to navigate to the page and then click **Add to Reading List** (⊕) to the left of the address bar. You can also add the current page to the Reading List by pressing Shift+⌘+D. To add all open tabs to the Reading List, click **Bookmarks** and then click **Add These Tabs to Reading List**. To add a link to the Reading List, press and hold Shift and click the link.

CHAPTER 3

Communicating via Email

OS X comes with the Apple Mail application that you can use to exchange email messages. After you type your account details into Mail, you can send email to friends, family, colleagues, and even total strangers almost anywhere in the world.

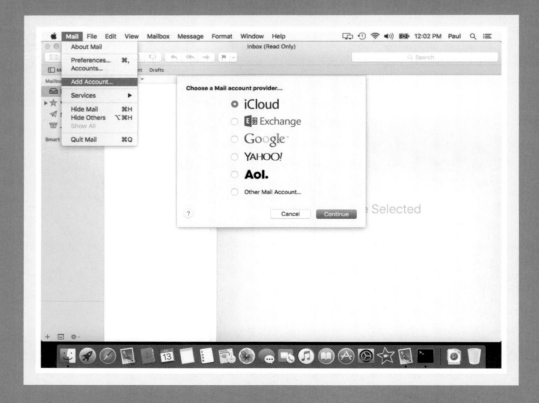

Add an Email Account

To send and receive email messages, you must add your email account to the Mail application. Your account is usually a POP (Post Office Protocol) account supplied by your Internet service provider, which should have sent you the account details. You can also use services such as Yahoo! and Gmail to set up a web-based email account, which enables you to send and receive messages from any computer. If you have an Apple ID — that is, an account for use on the Apple iCloud service (www.icloud.com) — you can also set up Mail with your Apple account details.

Add an Email Account

Get Started Adding an Account

1 In the Dock, click **Mail** (🥗).

2 Click **Mail**.

3 Click **Add Account**.

Note: If you are just starting Mail and the Welcome to Mail dialog is on-screen, you can skip steps **2** and **3**.

4 Click the type of account you are adding (⃝ changes to ⦿).

Ⓐ For a POP or IMAP account, click **Other Mail Account**.

5 Click **Continue**.

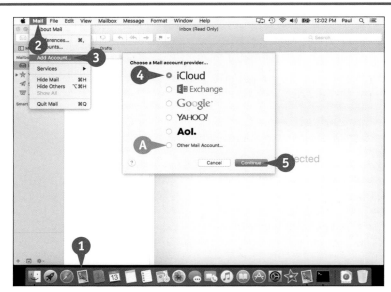

Add an iCloud Account

1 Type your Apple account address.

2 Type your Apple account password.

3 Click **Sign In**.

Mail signs in to your Apple account.

Note: Mail prompts you to choose which services you want to use with iCloud. See Chapter 14 to learn more.

4 Click **Add Account** (not shown).

Mail adds your Apple account.

Add a POP or IMAP Account

1 Type your name.

2 Type your account address.

3 Type your account password.

4 Click **Sign In**.

Note: If the sign-in is successful, you can skip the rest of the steps in this section.

5 Edit the User Name text as required.

6 Click the **Account Type** ⬍ and then click **POP** or **IMAP**.

7 Type the address of the account's incoming mail server.

8 Type the address of the account's outgoing mail server.

9 Click **Sign In**.

Mail signs in to your POP or IMAP account.

TIP

My email account requires me to use a nonstandard outgoing mail port. How do I set this up?
In the menu bar, click **Mail** and then **Preferences**. The Mail preferences appear. Click the **Accounts** tab. Click the **Outgoing Mail Server (SMTP)** ⬍ and then click **Edit SMTP Server List**. Click the outgoing mail server. Click the **Advanced** tab. Use the Port text box to type the nonstandard port number. Click **OK**. Click **Close** (⬤) and then click **Save**.

Send an Email Message

If you know the recipient's email address, you can send a message to that address. An email address is a set of characters that uniquely identifies the location of an Internet mailbox. Each address takes the form *username@domain*, where *username* is the name of the person's account with the ISP or with an organization, and *domain* is the Internet name of the company that provides the person's account. When you send a message, it travels through your ISP's outgoing mail server, which routes the messages to the recipient's incoming mail server, which then stores the message in the recipient's mailbox.

Send an Email Message

1 Click **New Message** (✐).

Note: You can also start a new message by pressing ⌘+N.

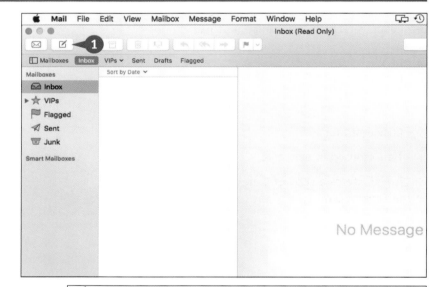

A message window appears.

2 Type the email address of the person to whom you are sending the message in the To field.

3 Type the email address of the person to whom you are sending a copy of the message in the Cc field.

Note: You can add multiple email addresses in both the To field and the Cc field by separating each address with a comma (,).

4 Type a brief description of the message in the Subject field.

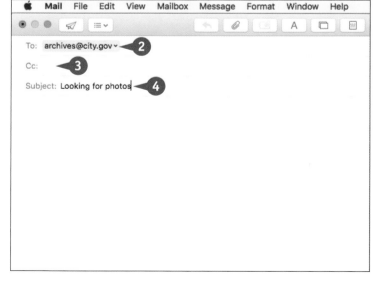

⑤ Type the message.

Ⓐ To change the message font, click **Fonts** (A) to display the Font panel.

Ⓑ To change the overall look of the message, click **Show Stationery** (▤) and then click a theme.

Note: Email is a text medium, so most people would rather not receive messages with extraneous graphics. It is best to keep your messages simple and unadorned. If you want to send messages without any graphics or text formatting, click **Format** and then click **Make Plain Text**.

⑥ Click **Send** (✐).

Mail sends your message.

Note: Mail stores a copy of your message in the Sent folder.

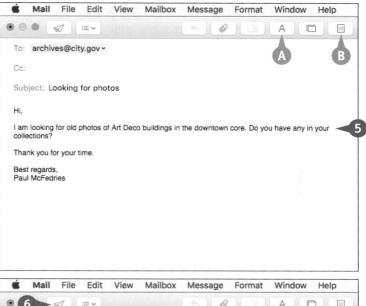

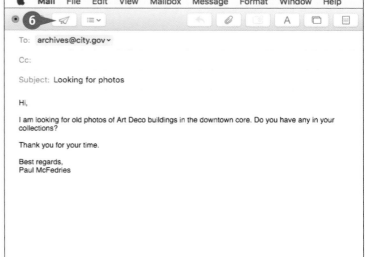

How can I compose a large number of messages offline?
You can compose your messages offline by following these steps: While disconnected from the Internet, click **Mail** (🗔) in the Dock to start Mail. To ensure you are working offline, click **Mailbox**. If the Take All Accounts Offline command is enabled, click that command. Compose and send the message. Each time you click **Send** (✐), your message is stored temporarily in the Outbox folder. When you are done, connect to the Internet. After a few moments, Mail automatically sends all the messages in the Outbox folder.

Add a File Attachment

If you have a file you want to send to another person, you can attach it to an email message. A typical message is fine for short notes, but you may have something more complex to communicate, such as budget numbers or a slide show, or some form of media that you want to share, such as an image.

These more complex types of data come in a separate file — such as a spreadsheet, presentation file, or picture file — so you need to send that file to your recipient. You do this by attaching the file to an email message.

Add a File Attachment

1 Click **New Message** (✐).

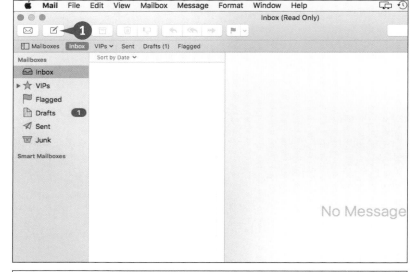

A message window appears.

2 Fill in the recipients, subject, and message text as described in the previous section, "Send an Email Message."

3 Press Return two or three times to move the cursor a few lines below your message.

4 Click **Attach** (⬚).

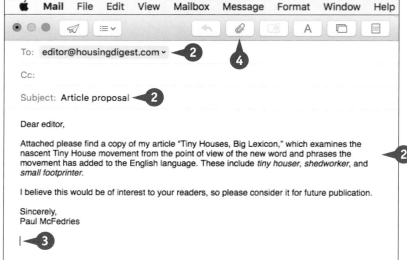

A file selection dialog appears.

5 Click the file you want to attach.

6 Click **Choose File**.

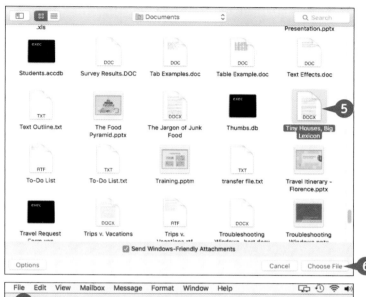

A Mail attaches the file to the message.

Note: Another way to attach a file to a message is to click and drag the file from Finder and drop it inside the message.

7 Repeat steps **4** to **6** to attach additional files to the message.

8 Click **Send** (✈).

Mail sends your message.

TIP

Is there a limit to the number of files I can attach to a message?
The number of files you can attach to the message has no practical limit. However, you should be careful with the total *size* of the files you send to someone. Many ISPs place a limit on the size of a message's attachments, which is usually between 2MB and 5MB. If you have an iCloud account, when you send a large attachment Mail asks if you want to use the Mail Drop feature, which stores the attachment in iCloud. Click **Use Mail Drop** to enable your recipient to download the attachment from iCloud.

Add a Signature Block

A *signature block* is a small amount of text that appears at the bottom of an email message. Instead of typing this information manually, you can save the signature in your Mail preferences. When you compose a new message, reply to a message, or forward a message, you can click a button to have Mail add the signature block to your outgoing message.

Signature blocks usually contain personal contact information, such as your phone numbers, business address, and email and website addresses. Mail supports multiple signature blocks, which is useful if you use multiple accounts or if you use Mail for different purposes such as business and personal.

Add a Signature Block

Create a Signature Block

1 Click **Mail**.

2 Click **Preferences**.

The Mail preferences appear.

3 Click **Signatures**.

4 Click the account for which you want to use the signature.

5 Click **Create a signature** (+).

Mail adds a new signature.

6 Type a name for the signature.

7 Type the signature text.

8 Repeat steps **4** to **7** to add other signatures, if required.

Note: You can add as many signatures as you want. For example, you may want to have one signature for business use and another for personal use.

9 Click **Close** (●).

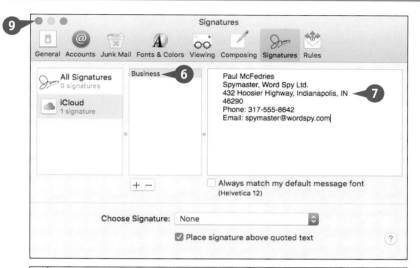

Insert the Signature

1 Click **New Message** (✏) to start a new message.

Note: To start a new message, see the section "Send an Email Message."

2 In the message text area, move the insertion point to the location where you want the signature to appear.

3 Click the **Signature** ⬦ and then click the signature you want to insert.

Ⓐ The signature appears in the message.

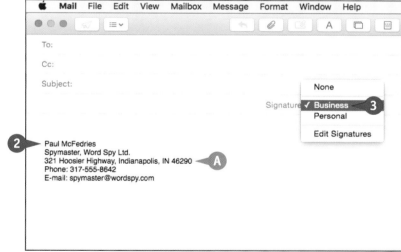

TIPS

I have multiple signatures. How can I choose which signature Mail adds automatically?
Follow steps **1** to **4** in the subsection "Create a Signature Block" to display the Signatures preferences and choose an account. Click the **Choose Signature** ⬦ and then click the signature you want to insert automatically into each message. If you prefer to add a signature manually, click **None**.

Can I format my signature text?
Yes. Follow steps **1** to **4** in the subsection "Create a Signature Block" to display the Signatures preferences and choose an account. Click the signature you want to modify and then use the commands on the Format menu to format your signature.

Receive and Read Email Messages

When another person sends you an email, that message ends up in your account mailbox on the incoming mail server maintained by your ISP or email provider. Therefore, you must connect to the incoming mail server to retrieve and read messages sent to you. You can do this using Mail, which takes care of the details behind the scenes. By default, Mail automatically checks for new messages while you are online, but you can also check for new messages at any time.

Receive and Read Email Messages

Receive Email Messages

1 Click **Get Mail** (⊠).

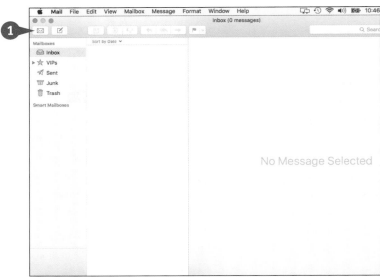

Ⓐ The Mail Activity area lets you know if you have any incoming messages.

Ⓑ If you have new messages, they appear in your Inbox folder with a blue dot in this column.

Ⓒ The Mail icon (📧) in the Dock shows the number of unread messages in the Inbox folder.

Read a Message

1 Click the message.

Mail displays the message text in the preview pane.

2 Read the message text in the preview pane.

Note: If you want to open the message in its own window, double-click the message.

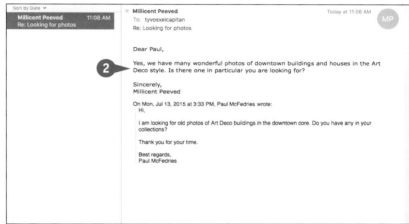

TIP

Can I change how often Mail automatically checks for messages?
Yes. Click **Mail** and then click **Preferences**. The Mail preferences appear. Click the **General** tab. Click the **Check for new messages** ⬦ and then click the time interval that you want Mail to use when checking for new messages automatically. If you do not want Mail to check for messages automatically, click **Manually** instead. Click **Close** (⬤) to close the Mail preferences.

Reply to a Message

When a message you receive requires a response — whether it is answering a question, supplying information, or providing comments — you can reply to that message. Most replies go only to the person who sent the original message. However, it is also possible to send the reply to all the people who were included in the original message's To and Cc lines. Mail includes the text of the original message in the reply, but you should edit the original message text to include only enough of the original message to put your reply into context.

Reply to a Message

1 Click the message to which you want to reply.

2 Click the reply type you want to use:

Click **Reply** (↩) to respond only to the person who sent the message.

Click **Reply All** (↞) to respond to all the addresses in the message's From, To, and Cc lines.

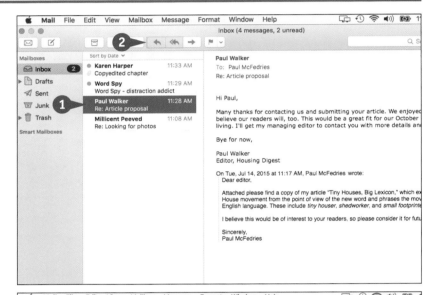

A message window appears.

Ⓐ Mail automatically inserts the recipient addresses.

Ⓑ Mail also inserts the subject line, preceded by Re:.

Ⓒ Mail includes the original message text at the bottom of the reply.

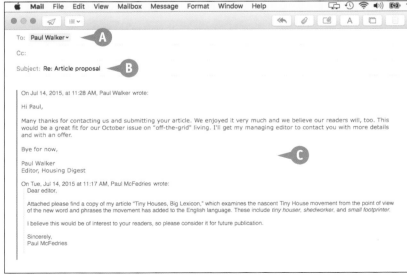

3 Edit the original message to include only the text relevant to your reply.

4 Click the area above the original message text.

To: Paul Walker ⌄

Cc:

Subject: Re: Article proposal

On Jul 14, 2015, at 11:28 AM, Paul Walker wrote:

Hi Paul,

Many thanks for contacting us and submitting your article. We enjoyed it very much and we believe our readers will, too. This would be a great fit for our October issue on "off-the-grid" living. I'll get my managing editor to contact you with more details and with an offer.

Bye for now,

Paul Walker
Editor, Housing Digest

5 Type your reply.

6 Click **Send** (✈).

Mail sends your reply.

Note: Mail stores a copy of your reply in the Sent folder.

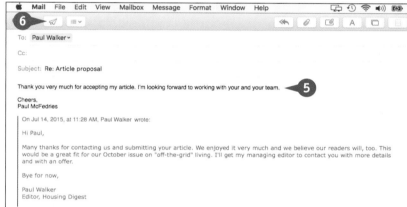

Mail   File   Edit   View   Mailbox   Message   Format   Window   Help

To: Paul Walker ⌄

Cc:

Subject: Re: Article proposal

Thank you very much for accepting my article. I'm looking forward to working with your and your team.

Cheers,
Paul McFedries

On Jul 14, 2015, at 11:28 AM, Paul Walker wrote:

Hi Paul,

Many thanks for contacting us and submitting your article. We enjoyed it very much and we believe our readers will, too. This would be a great fit for our October issue on "off-the-grid" living. I'll get my managing editor to contact you with more details and with an offer.

Bye for now,

Paul Walker
Editor, Housing Digest

TIP

I received a message inadvertently. Is there a way that I can pass it along to the correct recipient?
Yes. Mail comes with a feature that enables you to pass along inadvertent messages to the correct recipient. Click the message that you received inadvertently, click **Message**, and then click **Redirect** (or press Shift+⌘+E). Type the recipient's address and then click **Send**. Replies to this message will be sent to the original sender, not to you.

Forward a Message

If a message has information relevant to or that concerns another person, you can forward a copy of the message to that person. You can also include your own comments in the forward.

In the body of the forward, Mail includes the original message's addresses, date, and subject line. Below this information Mail also includes the text of the original message. In most cases, you will leave the entire message intact so your recipient can see it. However, if only part of the message is relevant to the recipient, you should edit the original message accordingly.

Forward a Message

1 Click the message that you want to forward.

2 Click **Forward** (➡).

Note: You can also press Shift+⌘+F.

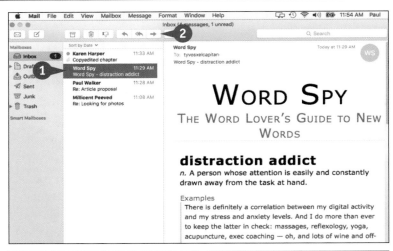

A message window appears.

Ⓐ Mail inserts the subject line, preceded by Fwd:.

Ⓑ The original message's addressees (To and From), date, subject, and text are included at the top of the forward.

3 Type the email address of the person to whom you are forwarding the message.

4 To send a copy of the forward to another person, type that person's email address in the Cc line.

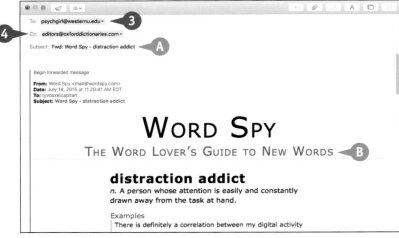

5 Edit the original message to include only the text relevant to your forward.

6 Click the area above the original message text.

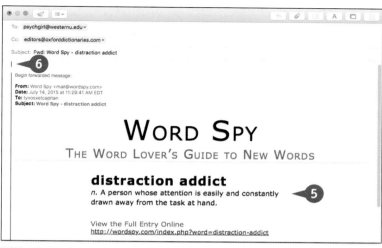

7 Type your comments.

8 Click **Send** (✈).

Mail sends your forward.

Note: Mail stores a copy of your forward in the Sent folder.

Note: You can forward someone a copy of the actual message rather than just a copy of the message text. Click the message, click **Message**, and then click **Forward As Attachment**. Mail creates a new message and includes the original message as an attachment.

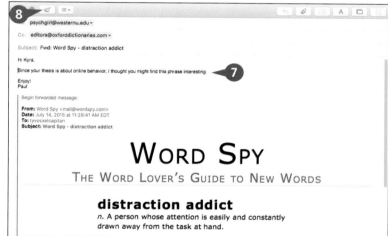

TIP

Mail always formats my replies as rich text, even when the original message is plain text. How can I fix this problem?
You can configure Mail to always reply using the same format as the original message. To do this, click **Mail** and then click **Preferences** to open the Mail preferences. Click the **Composing** tab. Click the **Use the same message format as the original message** check box (☐ changes to ☑) and then click **Close** (⬤) to close the Mail preferences.

Open and Save an Attachment

If you receive a message that has a file attached, you can open the attachment to view the contents of the file. However, although some attachments require only a quick viewing, other attachments may contain information that you want to keep. In this case, you should save these files to your Mac's hard drive so that you can open them later without having to launch Mail.

Be careful when dealing with attached files. Computer viruses are often transmitted by email attachments.

Open and Save an Attachment

Open an Attachment

① Click the message that has the attachment, as indicated by the Attachment symbol (⌀).

Ⓐ An icon appears for each message attachment.

② Double-click the attachment you want to open.

The file opens in the associated application.

Save an Attachment

1 Click the message that has the attachment, as indicated by the Attachment symbol (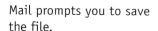).

2 Right-click the attachment you want to save.

3 Click **Save Attachment**.

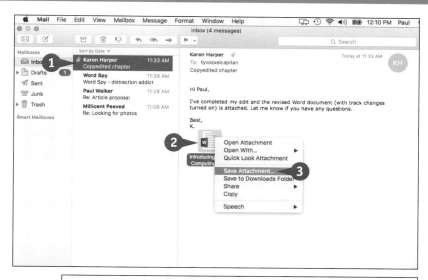

Mail prompts you to save the file.

4 Click in the Save As text box and edit the filename, if desired.

5 Click the **Where** ⬍ and select the folder into which you want the file saved.

6 Click **Save**.

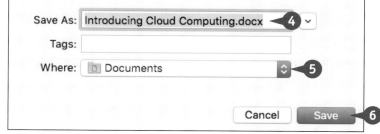

TIPS

Can I open an attachment using a different application?
In most cases, yes. OS X usually has a default application that it uses when you double-click a file attachment. However, it also usually defines one or more other applications capable of opening the file. To check this out, right-click the icon of the attachment you want to open and then click **Open With**. In the menu that appears, click the application that you prefer to use to open the file.

Are viruses a big problem on the Mac?
No, not yet. Most viruses target Windows PCs and only a few malicious programs target the Mac. However, as the Mac becomes more popular, expect to see more Mac-targeted virus programs. Therefore, you should still exercise caution when opening email attachments.

Create a Mailbox for Saving Messages

After you have used Mail for a while, you may find that you have many messages in your Inbox. To keep the Inbox uncluttered, you can create new mailboxes and then move messages from the Inbox to the new mailboxes.

You should use each mailbox you create to save related messages. For example, you could create separate mailboxes for people you correspond with regularly, projects you are working on, different work departments, and so on.

Create a Mailbox for Saving Messages

Create a Mailbox

1. Click **Mailbox**.

2. Click **New Mailbox**.

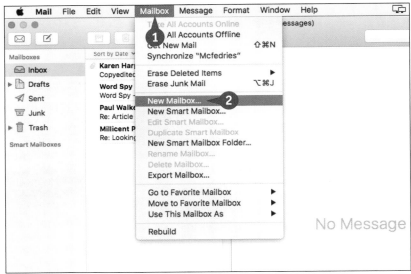

The New Mailbox dialog appears.

3. Click the **Location** and then click where you want the mailbox located.

4. Type the name of the new mailbox.

5. Click **OK**.

Ⓐ The new mailbox appears in the Mailboxes list.

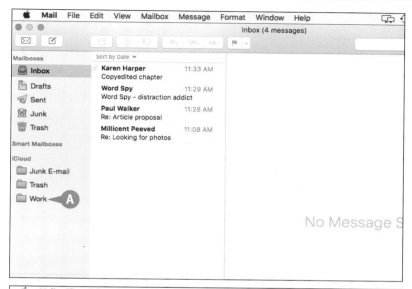

Move a Message to Another Mailbox

1 Position the mouse (🖈) over the message you want to move.

2 Click and drag the message and drop it on the mailbox to which you want to move it.

Mail moves the message.

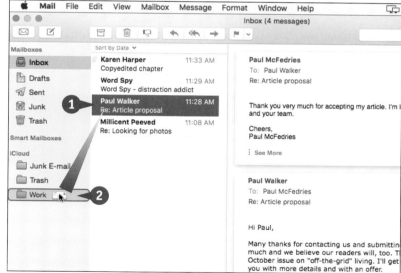

How do I rename a mailbox?
Right-click the mailbox and then click **Rename Mailbox**. Type the new name and then press `Return`. Note that Mail does not allow you to rename any of the built-in mailboxes, including Inbox, Drafts, and Trash.

How do I delete a mailbox?
Right-click the mailbox and then click **Delete**. When Mail asks you to confirm the deletion, click **Delete**. Note that Mail does not allow you to delete any of the built-in mailboxes, including Inbox, Drafts, and Trash. Remember, too, that when you delete a mailbox, you also delete any messages stored in that mailbox.

Add Events and Contacts from a Message

Y̶ou can save time and effort by adding items to Contacts and Calendar directly from Mail. As you learn in Chapter 6, you use the Contacts application to create new contacts, and you use the Calendar application to schedule new events. Quite often, however, you get the new information for a contact or an event from an email message you have received. Instead of using the cumbersome process of copying information from Mail to Contacts or Calendar, you can use Mail to add these new items directly.

Add Events and Contacts from a Message

1 Click the message that contains the contact data or event information.

A If Mail recognizes the data for either a contact or an event, it lets you know here.

2 Click **add** beside the data you want to enter.

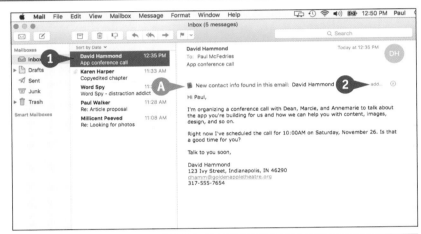

Mail displays the data.

3 If you are adding a contact, click **Add To Contacts**.

Note: If you are adding an event, click **Add To Calendar** instead.

Mail adds the contact or the event.

Process Messages Using Gestures

You can process your incoming Mail faster by using gestures to implement common tasks. With the Mail app on an iPhone or iPad, you can swipe right or left on a message to get quick access to a few message-related chores. That same convenience is also available in the OS X El Capitan Mail application. Using a trackpad or a Mighty Mouse, you can swipe right on a message to mark it as unread, and you can swipe left on a message to delete it.

Process Messages Using Gestures

Mark a Message as Unread

1 Swipe to the right on the message.

Note: If you are using a trackpad, use two fingers to swipe; if you are using a Mighty Mouse, use one finger to swipe.

2 Tap **Mark as Unread**.

Mail changes the message status to unread.

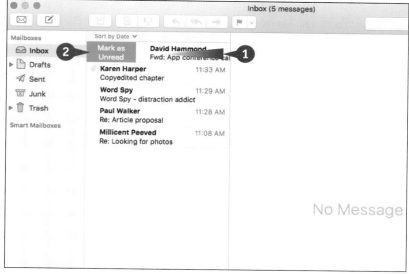

Delete a Message

1 Swipe to the left on the message.

2 Tap **Trash**.

Mail moves the message to the Trash folder.

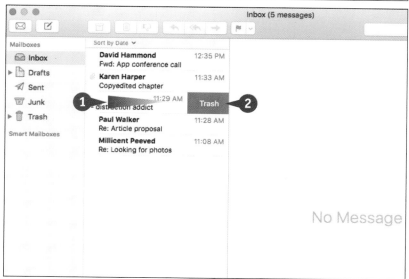

CHAPTER 4

Enhancing Online Privacy

This chapter helps you stay secure online by showing you a number of tasks designed to make your Internet sessions as safe and as private as possible. You learn how to delete your browsing history, prevent ad sites from tracking you online, browse the web privately, control junk email, and more.

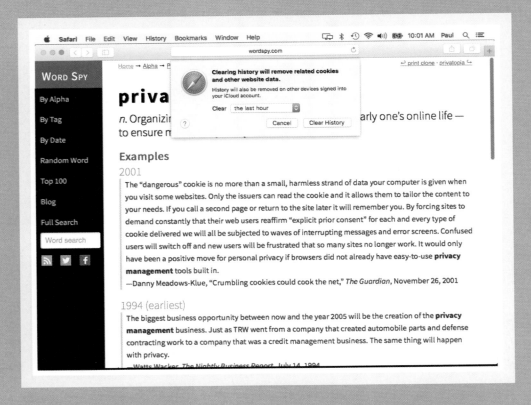

Delete a Site from Your Browsing History

You can enhance your privacy as well as the safety of other people who use your Mac by removing a private or dangerous site from your browsing history. Safari maintains your *browsing history*, which is a list of the sites you have visited. If you share your Mac with others, you might not want them to access certain private sites in your history. Similarly, if you accidentally stumble upon a dangerous or inappropriate site, you likely do not want others to see it. To help prevent both scenarios, you can delete the site from your browsing history.

Delete a Site from Your Browsing History

Delete a Single Site

1. Click **History**.

2. Click **Show History**.

   You can also run the Show History command by pressing ⌘+Y.

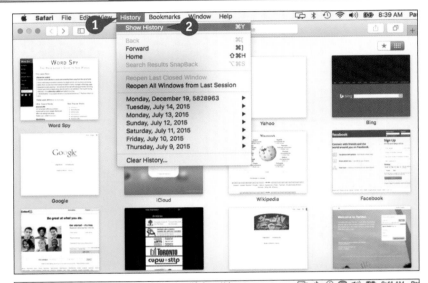

The History list appears.

3. Right-click the site you want to remove.

4. Click **Remove**.

Note: You can also click the site and then press Delete.

Safari deletes the site from your browsing history.

Note: To return to Safari, either click **History** and then **Hide History**, or press ⌘+Y.

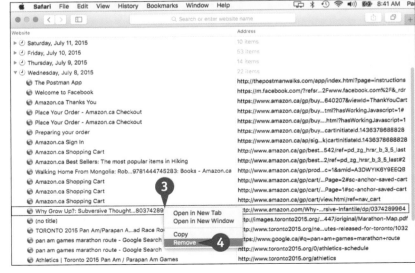

Delete an Entire Day

1 Click **History**.

2 Click **Show History**.

You can also run the Show History command by pressing ⌘+Y.

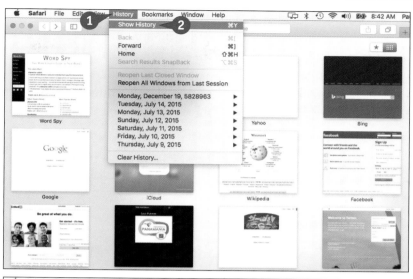

The History list appears.

3 Right-click the date you want to remove.

4 Click **Remove**.

Safari deletes the date from your browsing history.

Note: To return to Safari, either click **History** and then **Hide History**, or press ⌘+Y.

Note: To learn about the Clear History command, see section "Remove Saved Website Data," later in this chapter.

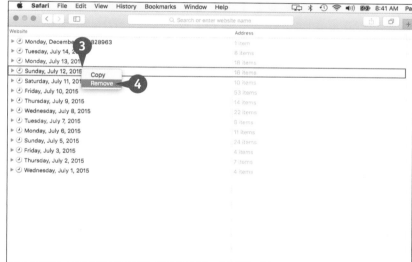

Is there a way to clear my browsing history automatically?

Yes. If you regularly delete all your browsing history, constantly running the Clear History command can become tiresome. Fortunately, you can configure Safari to make this chore automatic. Click **Safari** and then click **Preferences** to display the Safari preferences. Click the **General** tab. Click the **Remove history items** ⬦ and then click the length of time after which you want Safari to automatically remove an item from your browsing history. For example, if you click **After one day**, Safari clears out your browsing history daily.

Prevent Websites from Tracking You

You can prevent advertising sites from tracking your online movements by blocking the tracking files (called *cookies*) that they store on your Mac, as well as other mechanisms that they use for tracking users. Advertisers want to track the sites that you visit in order to deliver ads targeted to your likes and preferences. However, you cannot be sure how these sites are using the information they store about you. Therefore, many people prefer to configure Safari to prevent websites from using their tracking features. Note, however, that there is no guarantee as yet that websites will honor a so-called *Do Not Track* request.

Prevent Websites from Tracking You

1. Click **Safari**.
2. Click **Preferences**.

The Safari preferences appear.

3. Click the **Privacy** tab.

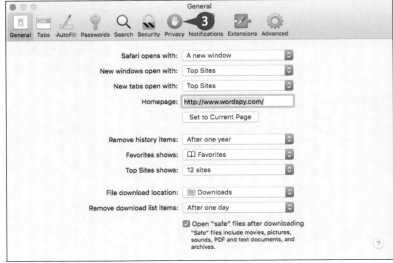

④ Click the **Allow from websites I visit** option (◯ changes to ⦿).

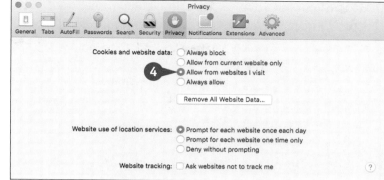

⑤ Click the **Ask websites not to track me** check box (☐ changes to ☑).

⑥ Click **Close** (⬤).

Safari no longer accepts cookies from third-party sites and sends all websites a Do Not Track request.

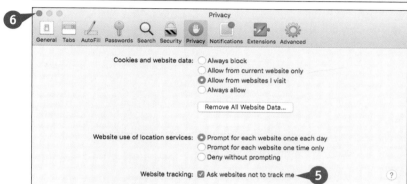

TIP

How can a website track me online?

Usually by using a *cookie*, a small text file that the website stores on your Mac. Cookies are used routinely by any website that needs to "remember" information about your session at that site, such as shopping cart and logon data.

A *third-party cookie* is set by a site other than the one you are viewing. An advertising site might store information about you in a third-party cookie and then use it to track your online activities. This works because the advertiser has ads on dozens or hundreds of websites, and that ad is the mechanism that enables the advertiser to set and read its cookie.

Remove Saved Website Data

To ensure that other people who have access to your Mac cannot view information from sites you have visited, you can delete Safari's saved website data.

Saving website data is useful because it enables you to quickly revisit a site. However, it is also dangerous because other people who use your Mac can just as easily visit or view information about those sites. This can be a problem if you visit financial sites, private corporate sites, or some other page that you would not want another person to visit. You reduce this risk by deleting your saved website data.

Remove Saved Website Data

1 Click **Safari**.

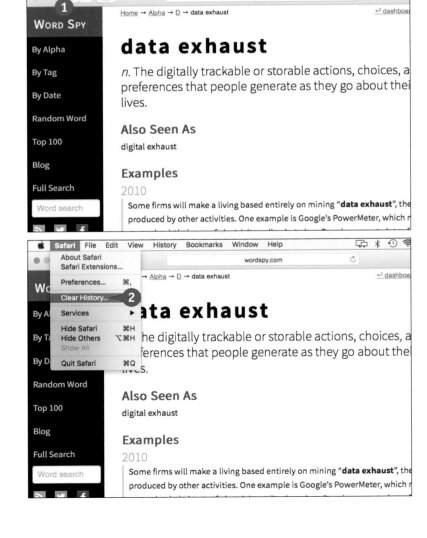

2 Click **Clear History**.

The Clear History dialog appears.

Note: Despite its name, the Clear History command removes not only your website history, but *all* your saved website data.

3 Click the **Clear** ⬍ and then click the history interval you want to remove.

4 Click **Clear History**.

Safari deletes the website data from the time interval you specified.

TIP

What types of website data does Safari save?

Besides your browsing history, the website data that Safari stores includes copies of page text, images, and other content so that sites load faster the next time you view them. Safari also tracks what sites you visit most often and uses that data to populate the Top Sites page that appears when you open a new tab or window.

Safari also saves the names of files you have downloaded, the names of websites that you have given permission to use your current location, and the names of websites that you have given permission to use the Notification Center.

Enable Private Browsing

If you regularly visit websites that contain sensitive or secret data, you can ensure that no one else sees any data for these sites by deleting Safari's saved website data, as described in the previous section, "Remove Saved Website Data." However, if these sites represent only a small percentage of the places you visit on the web, deleting all your website data is overkill. A better solution is to turn on Safari's Private Browsing feature before you visit private sites. This tells Safari to temporarily stop saving any website data. When you are ready to surf regular websites again, you can turn off Private Browsing to resume saving your website data.

Enable Private Browsing

1 Click **File**.

2 Click **New Private Window**.

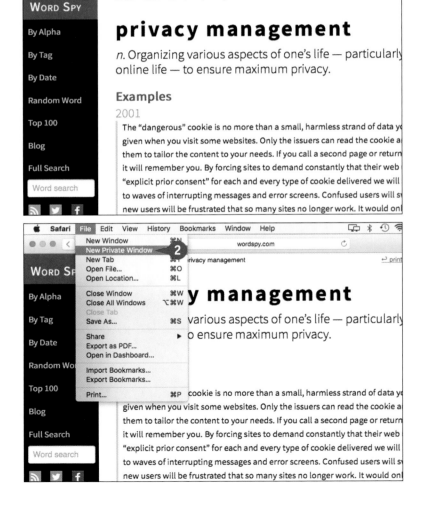

Safari creates a new window and activates the Private Browsing feature.

Ⓐ The address bar's dark background tells you that Private Browsing is turned on.

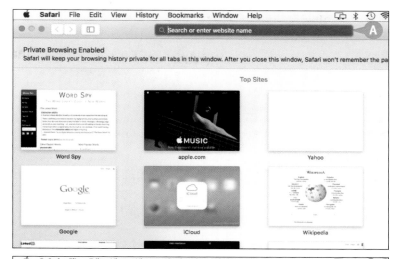

③ Visit the sites you want to see during your private browsing session.

④ When you are done, close the Private Browsing window.

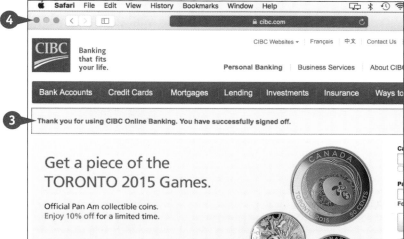

Can I prevent websites from requesting my location without having to activate Private Browsing?

Yes. Click **Safari** and then click **Preferences** to open the Safari preferences. Click the **Privacy** tab. In the Website Use of Location Services section, click the **Deny without prompting** option (◯ changes to ◉) and then click **Close** (●).

Safari's Search box displays suggestions based on my previous entries. Can I prevent this?

Yes. Click **Safari** and then click **Preferences** to open the Safari preferences. Click the **Search** tab. Click the **Include search engine suggestions** (☐ changes to ☑) check box, click the **Include Safari suggestions** (☐ changes to ☑) check box, and then click **Close** (●).

Delete a Saved Website Password

You can avoid unauthorized access to a website by removing the site's password that you saved earlier using Safari.

Many websites require a password, along with a username or email address. When you fill in this information and log on to the site, Safari offers to save the password so that you do not have to type it again when you visit the same page in the future. This is convenient, but it has a downside: Anyone who uses your Mac can also access the password-protected content. If you do not want this to happen, you can tell Safari to remove the saved password.

Delete a Saved Website Password

1 Click **Safari**.

2 Click **Preferences**.

The Safari preferences appear.

3 Click the **Passwords** tab.

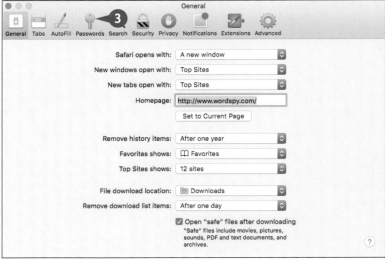

④ Click the web password you want to remove.

⑤ Click **Remove**.

Ⓐ If you no longer want Safari to save your website passwords, click the **AutoFill user names and passwords** check box (☑ changes to ☐).

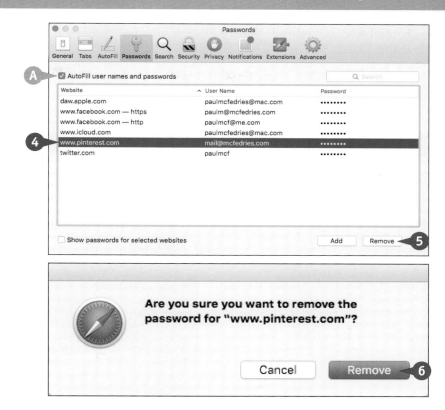

Safari asks you to confirm.

⑥ Click **Remove**.

Safari removes the password.

Are there any other website password security risks that I should know about?

Yes. Many websites offer to "remember" your login information. They do this by placing your username and password in a cookie stored on your Mac. Although convenient, it may lead to a problem: Other people who use your Mac to surf to the same sites can also access the password-protected content. To avoid this, be sure to click the website option (Ⓐ) that asks if you want to save your login data (☑ changes to ☐). Alternatively, set up separate user accounts for each person who uses your Mac, as described in Chapter 12.

Delete Saved Credit Card Data

You can avoid unauthorized use of your credit card by deleting card data that you saved earlier using Safari.

Most online purchases require a credit card, so retailers ask you to enter your card number and expiration date when you check out. To avoid the time and effort this requires, you can save your card data and have Safari enter it automatically each time you make a purchase. However, the downside to this convenience is that anyone who uses your Mac can also use your credit card information. To prevent this, you can delete the saved credit card data.

Delete Saved Credit Card Data

① Click **Safari**.

② Click **Preferences**.

The Safari preferences appear.

③ Click the **AutoFill** tab.

④ To the right of the Credit Cards check box, click **Edit**.

Safari displays the list of your
saved credit cards.

5 Click the credit card data you
want to remove.

6 Click **Remove**.

Safari removes the saved credit
card data.

7 Click **Done**.

Does Safari offer to save credit cards that I enter into a web form?
No, you must enter your credit card data by hand. To do this, click **Safari**, click **Preferences**, and then click
the **AutoFill** tab. Click **Edit** to the right of the Credit Cards check box to display the credit card list. Click
Add to create a new credit card entry. Type the credit card description, number, and expiry date, pressing
Tab after you fill in each field. Type the name that appears on the credit card and then click **Done**.

Move Spam to the Junk Mailbox Automatically

J unk email — or *spam* — refers to unsolicited, commercial email messages that advertise anything from baldness cures to cheap printer cartridges. Many spams advertise deals that are simply fraudulent, and others feature such unsavory practices as linking to adult-oriented sites, and sites that install spyware. Mail enables *junk mail filtering*, which looks for spam as it arrives in your Inbox and then marks each such message as junk. This enables you to quickly recognize junk mail and either delete it or move it to the Junk mailbox. However, you can customize Mail to automatically move all junk messages to the Junk mailbox.

Move Spam to the Junk Mailbox Automatically

1 Click **Mail**.

2 Click **Preferences**.

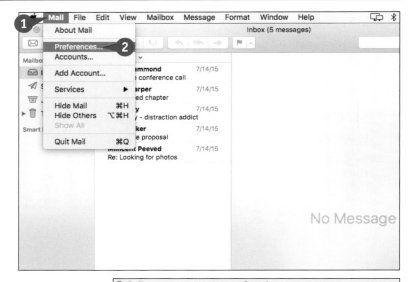

The Mail preferences appear.

3 Click the **Junk Mail** tab.

④ Click the **Move it to the Junk mailbox** option (○ changes to ◉).

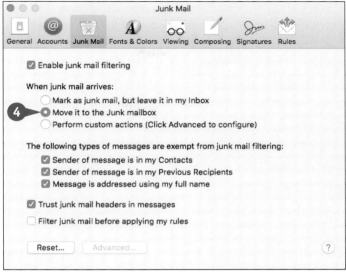

⑤ Click **Close** (●).

Mail closes the preferences and puts the new setting into effect.

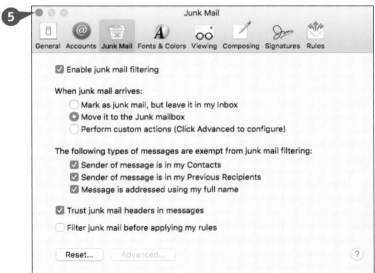

Why does Mail not mark some spam messages as junk?

Mail does not mark as junk any message addressed using your full name. To override this, click **Mail**, click **Preferences**, and then click the **Junk Mail** tab. Click the **Message is addressed using my full name** check box (☑ changes to ☐).

Is there a downside to automatically moving spam to the Junk mailbox?

Yes. Mail occasionally marks legitimate messages as junk. These are called *false positives*, and you should check for them by periodically opening the Junk mailbox. If you see one, click the message, click **Not Junk** in the preview pane, and then move the message to the Inbox.

Configure Advanced Junk Mail Filtering

You can gain greater control over Mail's junk mail filtering by configuring the advanced filtering options. These options are organized as a set of conditions that each message must meet before Mail marks it as junk, such as the sender not being in your contacts and the message containing spam content. The filtering options also specify a set of actions to perform on any message marked as junk, such as formatting the message with a special text color and moving it to the Junk mailbox. You can customize these options by deleting those you do not need and by adding new conditions and actions.

Configure Advanced Junk Mail Filtering

1 Click **Mail**.

2 Click **Preferences**.

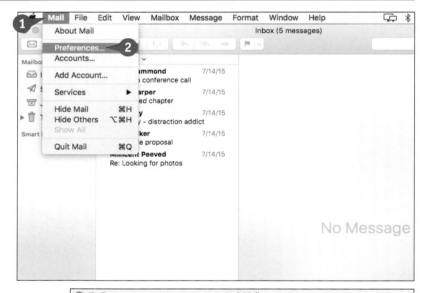

The Mail preferences appear.

3 Click the **Junk Mail** tab.

4 Click the **Perform custom actions** option (○ changes to ◉).

5 Click **Advanced**.

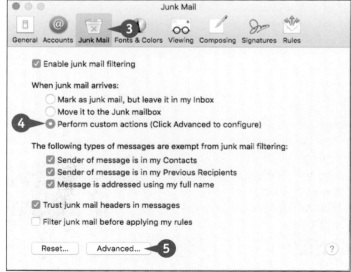

Safari displays the advanced junk mail filtering dialog.

A Mail marks a message as junk if it meets all these conditions.

6 Click a condition's **Remove** icon (−) to delete it.

7 Click an **Add** icon (⊕) to create a new condition.

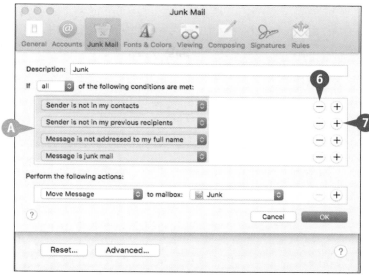

8 If you added a condition, use the pop-up menus and text box to define it.

9 Remove or add actions, as required.

10 Click **OK**.

Mail closes the dialog and puts the new filtering rules into effect.

11 Click **Close** (●).

Mail closes the preferences.

TIP

Almost all the spam I receive contains particular words in the subject or the message text. Can I set up junk mail filtering to handle this?
Yes. Click **Remove** (−) beside each existing condition. In the list of conditions, click **Add** (⊕). Click the first ⬦ and then click either **Subject** or **Message** content. In the second ⬦, click **contains**. In the text box, type the spam word. Repeat this procedure for each spam word you want include in your filter. Click the **If** ⬦ and then click **any** in the pop-up menu. Click **OK**.

Disable Remote Images

You can make your email address more private by thwarting the remote images inserted into some email messages. A *remote image* is an image that resides on an Internet server computer instead of being embedded in the email message. A special code in the message tells the server to display the image when you open the message. This is usually benign, but the same code can also alert the sender of the message that your email address is working. If the sender is a spammer, then this usually results in you receiving even more junk email. You can prevent this by disabling remote images.

Disable Remote Images

Disable Remote Images

① Click **Mail**.

② Click **Preferences**.

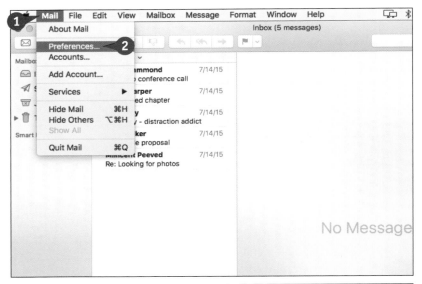

The Mail preferences appear.

③ Click the **Viewing** tab.

④ Click the **Load remote content in messages** check box (☑ changes to ☐).

⑤ Click **Close** (●).

Mail blocks remotes images in your messages.

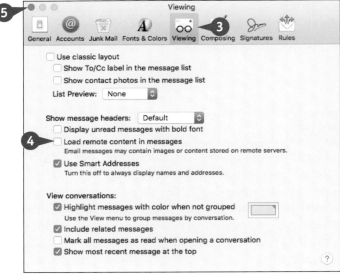

Display Remote Images in a Message

1 Click a message.

A Mail displays a placeholder for each remote image.

2 Click **Load Remote Content**.

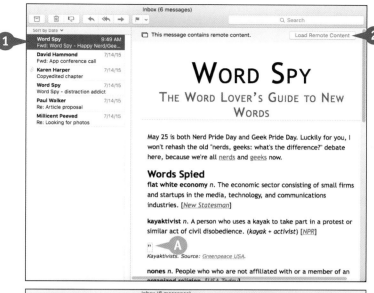

B Mail displays the message's remote images.

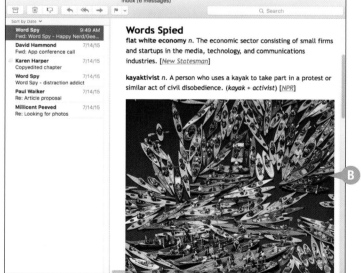

How do remote images cause me to receive more spam?

Many spammers include in their messages a *web bug*, which is a small and usually invisible image, the code for which is inserted into the email message. That code specifies a remote address from which to download the web bug when you display the message. However, the code also includes a reference to your email address. The remote server notes that you received the message, which means your address is a working one and is therefore a good target for further spam messages. By blocking remote images, you also block web bugs, which means you undermine this confirmation and so receive less spam.

CHAPTER 5

Talking via Messages and FaceTime

OS X comes with the Messages application, which you use to exchange instant messages with other OS X users, as well as anyone with an iPhone, iPad, or iPod touch. You can use FaceTime to make video calls.

Sign In to Messages

OS X includes the Messages application to enable you to use the iMessage technology to exchange instant messages with other people who are online. The first time you open Messages, you might be required to sign in with your Apple ID. Note that signing in is optional. You can still use Messages with other instant messaging services such as AIM, Google, or Yahoo!, even if either you do not have an Apple ID or you have an Apple ID but are not signed in.

Sign In to Messages

1 Click **Messages** (💬).

The iMessage dialog appears.

A If you do not have or do not want to use an Apple ID with Messages, click **Not Now** and skip the rest of the steps in this section.

2 Type your Apple ID.

iMessage

Sign in with your Apple ID to send unlimited messages to any Mac, iPhone, iPad, or iPod touch right from your Mac.

Apple ID: tyvosxelcapitan@mcfedries.
Password: required

Not Now   Sign in

Create new Apple ID...   Forgot Apple ID or password?

③ Type your Apple ID password.

④ Click **Sign in**.

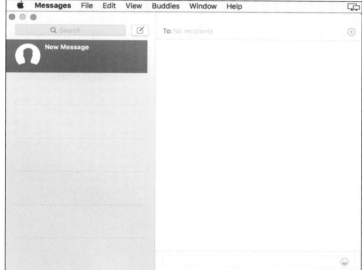

The Messages window appears.

What if I do not have an Apple ID?

You can create a new Apple ID during the sign-in process. After you click **Messages** (💬) and the iMessage dialog appears, click **Create new Apple ID**. OS X opens Safari, which takes you to the Create an Apple ID page. Type your name, the email address you want to use as your Apple ID, and the password you want to use. You must also choose several security questions, specify your birthday and address, and provide a rescue email address. Click **Create Apple ID** to complete the operation.

Send a Message

In the Messages application, an instant messaging conversation is most often the exchange of text messages between two or more people who are online and available to chat.

An instant messaging conversation begins with one person inviting another person to exchange messages. In Messages, this means sending an initial instant message, and the recipient either accepts or rejects the invitation.

Send a Message

1 Click **Compose new message** (✐).

Note: You can also click **File** and then click **New Message**, or press ⌘+N.

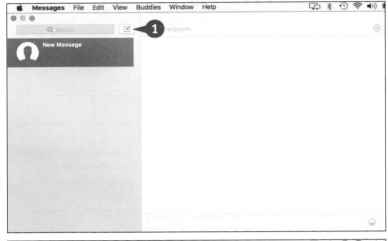

Messages begins a new conversation.

2 In the To field, type the message recipient using one of the following:

The person's email address.

The person's mobile phone number.

The person's name, if that person is in your Contacts list.

Ⓐ You can also click **Add Contact** (⊕) to select a name from your Contacts list.

3 Type your message.

B You can also click 😊 if you want to insert an emoji symbol into your message.

4 Press **Return**.

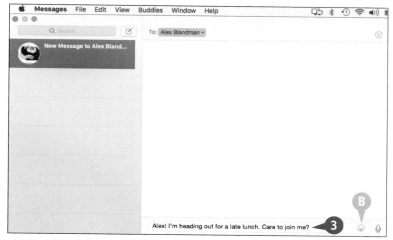

Messages sends the text to the recipient.

C The recipient's response appears in the transcript window.

D You see the ellipsis symbol (⋯) when the other person is typing.

5 Repeat steps **3** and **4** to continue the conversation.

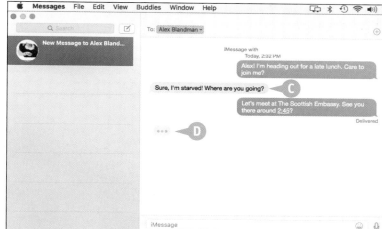

TIPS

What is an emoji?

An *emoji* is a pictograph similar to a smiley or emoticon. Many emojis represent an emotional state, such as happy, sad, or angry. There are also many emojis that show symbols such as flowers or animals that you can use to add a bit of visual interest to your messages.

How do I make the Messages text a bit bigger?

To change the size of the text that appears in the Messages window, click **Messages** and then click **Preferences**. In the Messages preferences, click the **General** tab. Drag the **Text size** slider to the right to make the text bigger, or to the left to make the text smaller.

Send a File in a Message

If, during an instant messaging conversation, you realize you need to send someone a file, you can save time by sending the file directly from the Messages application.

When you need to send a file to another person, your first thought might be to attach that file to an email message. However, if you happen to be in the middle of an instant messaging conversation with that person, it is easier and faster to use Messages to send the file. Note that not all instant message services support sending files.

Send a File in a Message

1 Start the conversation with the person to whom you want to send the file.

2 Click **Buddies**.

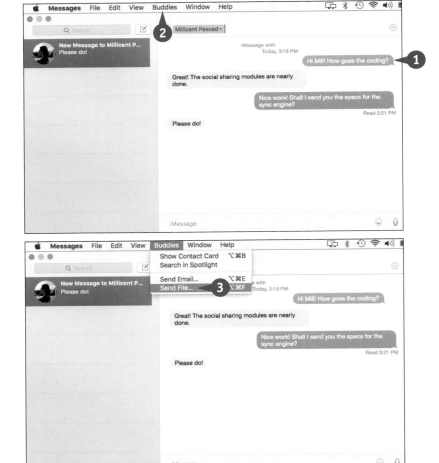

3 Click **Send File**.

Note: You can also press .

Messages displays a file selection dialog.

④ Click the file you want to send.

⑤ Click **Send**.

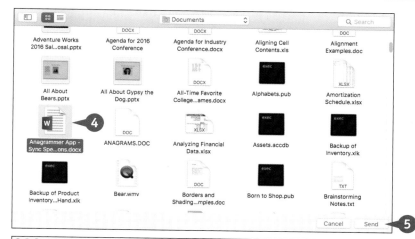

Ⓐ Messages adds an icon for the file to the message box.

⑥ Type your message.

⑦ Press Return.

Messages sends the message and adds the file as an attachment.

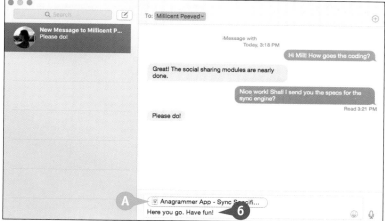

TIP

How do I save a file that I receive during a conversation?
When you receive a message that has a file attachment, the message shows the name of the file, with the file's type icon to the left. Right-click the file attachment and then click **Save to Downloads** to save the file to your Downloads folder. Messages saves the file and then displays the Downloads folder.

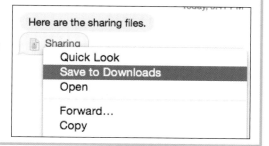

Sign In to FaceTime

FaceTime is a video and audio chat feature that enables you to see and speak to another person over the Internet. To use FaceTime to conduct video chats with your friends, you must each first sign in using your Apple ID. This could be an iCloud account that uses the Apple icloud.com address, or it could be your existing email address.

After you create your Apple ID, you can use it to sign in to FaceTime. Note that you only have to do this once. In subsequent sessions, FaceTime automatically signs you in.

Sign In to FaceTime

1 In the Dock, click **FaceTime** ( ).

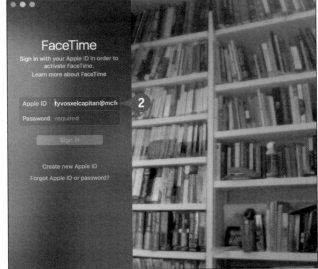

The FaceTime window appears.

2 Type your Apple ID email address.

③ Type your Apple ID password.

④ Click **Sign in**.

FaceTime verifies your Apple ID
and then displays the regular
FaceTime window.

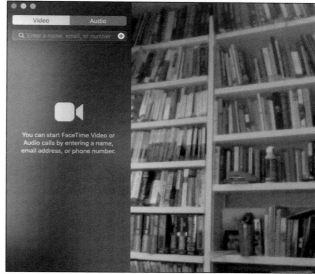

TIPS

What equipment do I and the person I am calling need to use FaceTime?

For video calls, your Mac must have a web camera, such as the iSight camera that comes with many Macs. For both video and audio calls, your Mac must have a microphone, such as the microphone that is part of the iSight camera.

Which devices support FaceTime?

You can use FaceTime on any Mac running OS X 10.6.6 or later. For OS X Snow Leopard (10.6.6), FaceTime is available through the App Store for 99 cents. For later versions of OS X, FaceTime is installed by default. FaceTime is also an app that runs on the iPhone 4 and later, the iPad 2 and later, and the iPod touch fourth generation and later.

Connect Through FaceTime

nce you sign in with your Apple ID, you can use the FaceTime application to connect with another person and conduct a video or audio chat. You connect using whatever email address or phone number the person has associated with her FaceTime account. FaceTime will attempt to connect to that person on any of her devices, which can include a Mac, an iPhone, an iPad touch, or an iPad.

Connect Through FaceTime

1 Begin typing the name of the contact or the phone number you want to call.

A Contacts that support FaceTime calling appear with the FaceTime icon (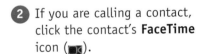).

2 If you are calling a contact, click the contact's **FaceTime** icon (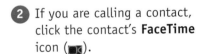).

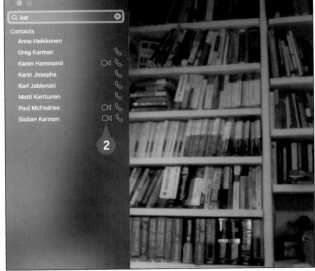

FaceTime sends a message to the contact asking if he or she would like a FaceTime connection.

③ The other person must click or tap **Accept** to complete the connection.

FaceTime connects with the other person.

Ⓑ The other person's video takes up the bulk of the FaceTime screen.

Ⓒ Your video appears in the picture-in-picture (PiP) window.

Note: You can click and drag the PiP to a different location within the FaceTime window.

④ When you finish your FaceTime call, click **End**.

TIP

Can I use FaceTime to call a person without using video?
Yes, FaceTime also supports audio calls, which is useful if the other person does not have a device that supports FaceTime, or if you feel you do not know the other person well enough to place a video call. Use FaceTime to start typing the person's name and then click the **Audio** icon (🔊) that appears to the right of the person's name. If you have an iPhone running iOS 8 or later nearby, then you can click the phone number that appears below the Call Using iPhone text; otherwise, click **FaceTime Audio**.

CHAPTER 6

Tracking Contacts and Events

In OS X, you use the Contacts application to manage your contacts by storing information such as phone numbers, email addresses, street addresses, and much more. You also use the Calendar application to enter and track events and to-do items.

Add a New Contact

OS X includes the Contacts application for managing information about the people you know, whether they are colleagues, friends, or family members. The Contacts app refers to these people as *contacts*, and you store each person's data in an object called a *card*. Each card can store a wide variety of information. For example, you can store a person's name, company name, phone numbers, email address, instant messaging data, street address, notes, and much more. Although you will mostly use Contacts cards to store data about people, you can also use a card to keep information about companies.

Add a New Contact

1 In the Dock, click **Contacts** (📖).

2 Click **File**.

3 Click **New Card**.

Ⓐ You can also begin a new contact by clicking **Add** (+) and then clicking **New Contact**.

Note: You can also invoke the New Card command by pressing ⌘+N.

Ⓑ Contacts adds a new card.

4 In the First field, type the contact's first name.

5 In the Last field, type the contact's last name.

6 In the Company field, type the contact's company name.

7 If the contact is a company, click the **Company** check box (☐ changes to ☑).

8 In the first Phone field, click ↕ and then click the category you want to use.

9 Type the phone number.

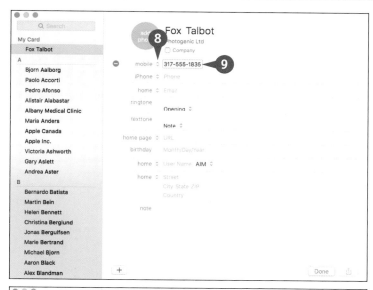

10 Repeat steps **8** and **9** to enter data in some or all of the other fields.

Note: To learn how to add more fields to the card, see the next section, "Edit a Contact."

11 Click **Done**.

Contacts saves the new card.

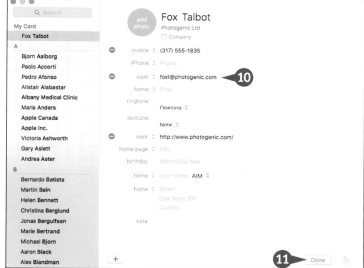

TIP

If I include a contact's email address, is there a way to send that person a message without having to type the address?

Yes. Click the contact's card, click the email address category (such as **work** or **home**), and then click **Send Email**. Mail displays a new email message with the contact already added in the To field. Fill in the rest of the message as required and then click **Send** (✈).

Edit a Contact

If you need to make changes to the information already in a contact's card, or if you need to add new information to a card, you can edit the card from within Contacts. The default fields you see in a card are not the only types of data you can store for a contact. Contacts offers a large number of extra fields. These include useful fields such as Middle Name, Nickname, Job Title, Department, URL (web address), and Birthday. You can also add extra fields for common data items such as phone numbers, email addresses, and dates.

Edit a Contact

1 Click the card you want to edit.

2 Click **Edit**.

A Contacts makes the card's fields available for editing.

3 Edit the existing fields as required.

4 To add a field, click an empty placeholder and then type the field data.

5 To remove a field, click **Delete** (➖).

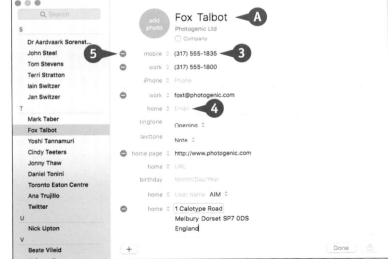

6 To add a new field type, click
Card.

7 Click **Add Field**.

8 Click the type of field you want.

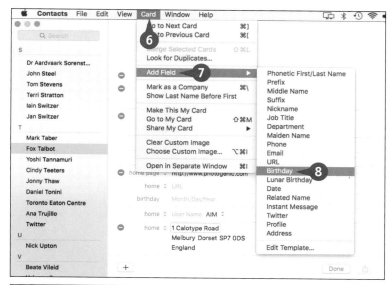

B Contacts adds the field to
the card.

9 When you complete your edits,
click **Done**.

Contacts saves the edited card.

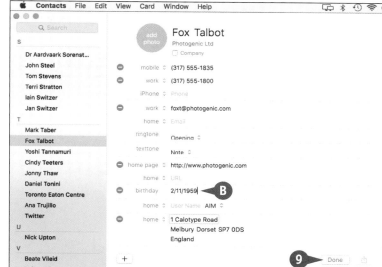

TIP

How do I add a picture for the new contact?

Click the contact's card and then drag a photo from Finder and drop it on the contact's picture box. Drag
the preview to the position you want, click + or − to adjust the magnification, and then click **Done**.

Alternatively, click the contact's picture box and then click **edit**. A dialog of picture options appears. Click
the type of picture you want to add: Defaults, iCloud Photos, Faces, or Camera. Click or take the picture and
then click **Done** to close the picture dialog.

Create a Contact Group

You can organize your contacts into one or more groups, which is useful for viewing just a subset of your contacts. For example, you could create separate groups for friends, family, work colleagues, or business clients. Groups are handy if you have many contacts in your address book. By creating and maintaining groups, you can navigate your contacts more easily. You can also perform groupwide tasks, such as sending a single email message to everyone in the group. You can create a group first and then add members, or you can select members in advance and then create the group.

Create a Contact Group

Create a Contact Group

1 Click **File**.

2 Click **New Group**.

Note: You can also run the New Group command by pressing Shift + ⌘ + N.

A Contacts displays the lists of groups and adds a new group.

3 Type a name for the group.

4 Press Return.

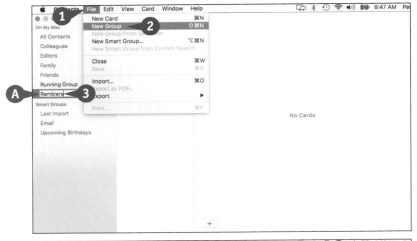

5 Click **All Contacts**.

6 Click and drag a contact to the group.

Contacts adds the contact to the group.

7 Repeat step **6** for the other contacts you want to add to the group.

Create a Group of Selected Contacts

1 Select the contacts you want to include in the new group.

Note: To select multiple contacts, press and hold ⌘ and click each card.

2 Click **File**.

3 Click **New Group From Selection**.

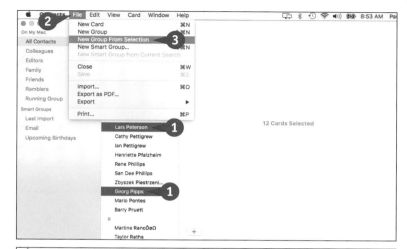

B Contacts adds a new group.

C Contacts adds the selected contacts as group members.

4 Type a name for the group.

5 Press Return.

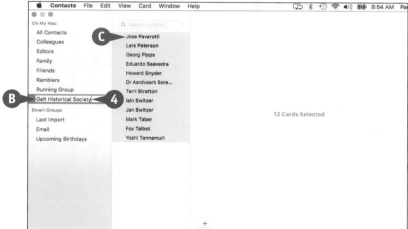

TIPS

Can I send an email message to the group?

Yes. With a group, you send a single message to the group, and Mail automatically sends a copy to each member. Right-click the group and then click **Send Email to "*Group*,"** where *Group* is the name of the group.

What is a Smart Group?

It is a group where each member has one or more fields in common, such as the company name or city. When you create the Smart Group, you specify one or more criteria, and then Contacts automatically adds members to the group who meet those criteria. Click **File**, click **New Smart Group**, and then enter your group criteria.

Navigate the Calendar

Calendar enables you to create and work with events, which are either scheduled appointments or activities such as meetings and lunches, or all-day activities such as birthdays or vacations. Before you create an event, you must first select the date on which the event occurs. You can do this in Calendar by navigating the built-in calendar or by specifying the date that you want.

Calendar also lets you change the calendar view to suit your needs. For example, you can show just a single day's worth of events or a week's worth of events.

Navigate the Calendar

Using the Calendar

1 In the Dock, click **Calendar** (🗓).

2 Click **Month**.

3 Click **Next Month** (❯) until the month of your event appears.

A If you go too far, click **Previous Month** (❮) to move back to the month you want.

B To see a specific date, click the day and then click **Day** (or press ⌘+**1**).

C To see a specific week, click any day within the week and then click **Week** (or press ⌘+**2**).

D To return to viewing the entire month, click **Month** (or press ⌘+**3**).

E If you want to return to today's date, click **Today** (or press ⌘+**T**).

Go to a Specific Date

1 Click **View**.

2 Click **Go to Date**.

Note: You can also select the Go to Date command by pressing Shift + ⌘ + T.

The Go to Date dialog appears.

3 In the Date text box, type the date you want using the format mm/dd/yyyy.

F You can also click the month, day, or year and then click ⌃ to increase or decrease the value.

4 Click **Show**.

5 Click **Day**.

G Calendar displays the date.

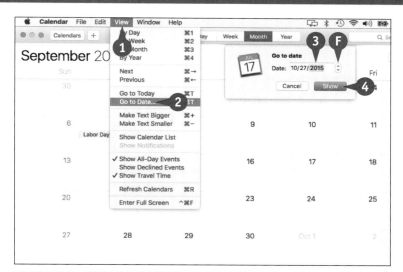

TIP

In the Week view, the week begins on Sunday. How can I change this to Monday?

Calendar's default Week view has Sunday on the left and Saturday on the right. To display the weekend days together, with Monday on the left signaling the start of the week, follow these steps: Click **Calendar** in the menu bar and then click **Preferences**; the Calendar preferences appear. Click the **General** tab. Click the **Start week on** ⌃, select **Monday** from the pop-up menu, and then click **Close** (●).

Create an Event

You can help organize your life by using Calendar to record your events — such as appointments, meetings, phone calls, and dates — on the date and time they occur.

If the event has a set time and duration — for example, a meeting or a lunch date — you add the event directly to the calendar as a regular appointment. If the event has no set time — for example, a birthday, anniversary, or multiple-day event such as a convention or vacation — you can create an all-day event.

Create an Event

Create a Regular Event

1 Navigate to the date when the event occurs.

2 Click **Calendars**.

3 Click the calendar you want to use.

4 Double-click the time when the event starts.

Note: If the event is less than or more than an hour, you can also click and drag the mouse (🖑) over the full event period.

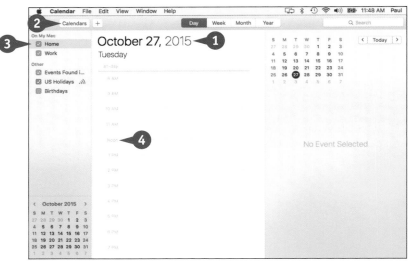

Ⓐ Calendar adds a one-hour event.

5 Type the name of the event.

6 Press **Return**.

Create an All-Day Event

1 Click **Week**.

2 Navigate to the week that includes the date when the event occurs.

3 Click **Calendars**.

4 Click the calendar you want to use.

5 Double-click anywhere inside the event date's all-day section.

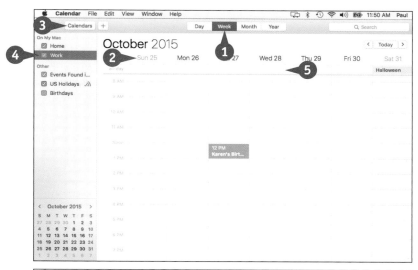

B Calendar adds a new all-day event.

6 Type the name of the event.

7 Press [Return].

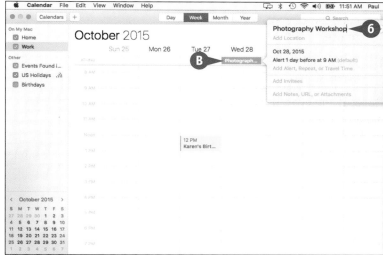

TIP

How can I specify event details such as the location and a reminder message?

Follow the steps in this section to create an event and then double-click the event. Type the location of the event in the Add Location text box. Click the event's date or time, click **alert**, and then click the amount of time before the event that you want to receive the reminder. To add notes, attach a file, or add a web address, click **Add Notes, URL, or Attachments** and then click the type of information you want to add. Click outside the event. Calendar saves the new event configuration.

Create a Repeating Event

If you have an activity or event that recurs at a regular interval, you can create an event and configure it to repeat in Calendar automatically. This saves you from having to add the future events repeatedly yourself because Calendar adds them for you.

You can repeat an event daily, weekly, monthly, or yearly. For even greater flexibility, you can set up a custom interval. For example, you could have an event repeat every five days, every second Friday, on the first Monday of every month, and so on.

Create a Repeating Event

1 Create an event.

Note: To create an event, follow the steps in the previous section, "Create an Event."

2 Double-click the event.

Calendar displays information for the event.

3 Click the event's date and time.

Calendar opens the event for editing.

4 Click the **repeat ↕**.

5 Click the interval you want to use.

Ⓐ If you want to specify a custom interval such as every two weeks or the first Monday of every month, click **Custom** and configure your interval in the dialog that appears.

6 Press **Return**.

Ⓑ Calendar adds the repeating events to the calendar.

TIPS

How do I configure an event to stop after a certain number of occurrences?

Follow steps **1** to **5** to select a recurrence interval. Click the **end repeat ↕** and then select **After** from the pop-up menu. Type the number of occurrences you want. Click outside the event.

Can I delete a single occurrence from a recurring series of events?

Yes, you can delete one occurrence from the calendar without affecting the rest of the series. Click the occurrence you want to delete, and then press **Delete**. Calendar asks whether you want to delete all the occurrences or just the selected occurrence. Click **Delete Only This Event**.

Send or Respond to an Event Invitation

You can include other people in your event by sending them invitations to attend. If you receive an event invitation yourself, you can respond to it to let the person organizing the event know whether you will attend.

If you have an event that requires other people, Calendar has a feature that enables you to send invitations to other people who use a compatible email program. The advantage of this approach is that when other people respond to the invitation, Calendar automatically updates the event. If you receive an event invitation yourself, the email message contains buttons that enable you to respond quickly.

Send or Respond to an Event Invitation

Send an Event Invitation

1 Create an event.

Note: To create an event, follow the steps in the section "Create an Event."

2 Double-click the event.

3 Click **Add Invitees**.

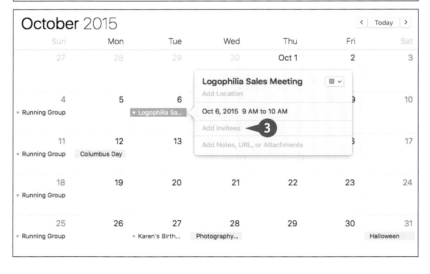

4 Begin typing the name of a person you want to invite.

5 Click the person you want to invite.

6 Repeat steps **4** and **5** to add more invitees.

7 Click **Send**.

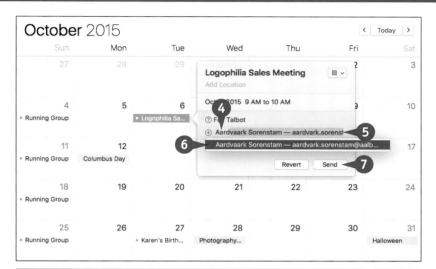

Handle an Event Invitation

A The Invitation button shows the number of pending invitations you have received via iCloud.

B The event appears tentatively in your calendar.

1 Click **Invitation** (⬇).

2 Click the button that represents your reply to the invitation:

C Click **Accept** if you can attend the event.

D Click **Decline** if you cannot attend the event.

E Click **Maybe** if you are currently not sure whether you can attend.

TIPS

Is it possible to see emailed invitations in Calendar before I decide whether to accept them?

Yes. Open Mail, click **Mail** in the menu bar, click **Preferences**, click **General**, click the **Add invitations to Calendar** ⬦, and then click **Automatically**. Events you have not responded to appear in gray in the calendar.

How do I know when a person has accepted or declined an invitation?

Double-click the event. In the list of invitees, you see a check mark beside each person who has accepted the invitation; you see a question mark beside each person who has not made a choice or who has selected Maybe; and you see a red Not symbol beside each person who has declined the invitation.

CHAPTER 7

Playing and Organizing Music

You can use iTunes to create a library of music and use that library to play songs, albums, and collections of songs called playlists. You can also purchase music from the iTunes Store and more.

Understanding the iTunes Library

O S X includes iTunes to enable you to play back and manage various types of audio files. iTunes also includes features for organizing and playing videos, watching movies and TV shows, and organizing apps, but iTunes is mostly concerned with audio-related media and content.

Most of your iTunes time will be spent in the library, so you need to understand the various categories — such as music and audiobooks — that iTunes uses to organize the library's audio content. You also need to know how to configure the library to show only the categories with which you will be working.

The iTunes Library

The iTunes library is where your Mac stores the files that you can play and work with in the iTunes application. Although iTunes has some video components, its focus is on audio features, so most of the library sections are audio-related. These sections enable you to work with music, podcasts, audiobooks, ringtones, and Internet radio.

Understanding Library Categories

The Sources section in the upper left corner of the iTunes window displays the various categories that are available in the iTunes library. The audio-related categories include Music, Podcasts, Books (for audiobooks), Tones, and Internet Radio.

Each category shows you the contents of that category and the details for each item. For example, in the Music category, you can see details such as the name of each album and the artist who recorded it.

Configuring the Library

You can configure which categories of the iTunes library appear in the Library list on the left side of the iTunes window. Click **More** (•••) and then click **Edit**. Click the check box for each type of content you want to work with (☐ changes to ☑) and then click **Done**.

Navigate the iTunes Window

Familiarizing yourself with the various elements of the iTunes window is a good idea so that you can easily navigate and activate elements when you are ready to play audio files, music CDs, or podcasts; import and burn audio CDs; create your own playlists; or listen to Internet radio. In particular, you need to learn the iTunes playback controls because you will use them to control the playback of almost all music you work with in iTunes.

A Playback Controls

These buttons control media playback and enable you to adjust the volume.

B Status Area

This area displays information about the item currently playing or the action that iTunes is currently performing.

C Sources

Click the buttons in this section to select the type of content you want to view.

D Sort List

The commands in this list sort the contents of the current iTunes category.

E iTunes Store

Click this command to access the iTunes Store, which enables you to purchase songs and albums, subscribe to podcasts, and more.

F Contents

The contents of the current iTunes library source appear here.

Play a Song

You use the Music category of the iTunes library to play a song that is stored on your computer. Although iTunes offers several methods to locate the song you want to play, the easiest method is to display the albums you have in your iTunes library, and then open the album that contains the song you want to play. While the song is playing, you can control the volume to suit the music or your current location. If you need to leave the room or take a call, you can pause the song currently playing.

Play a Song

1. Click **Music** (♫).

2. Open the sort list and click **Albums**.

   You can also click a sort option such as Songs, Artists, or Genres.

3. Click the **Sort by** ⬙ and then click **Artist**.

4. Click the album that contains the song you want to play.

Ⓐ If you want to play the entire album, click **Play** (▶).

5. Double-click the song you want to play.

iTunes begins playing the song.

Ⓑ Information about the song playback appears here.

Ⓒ iTunes displays a speaker icon (🔊) beside the currently playing song.

Ⓓ If you need to stop the song temporarily, click **Pause** (⏸).

Note: You can also pause and restart a song by pressing the **Spacebar**.

Ⓔ You can use the Volume slider to adjust the volume (see the Tip).

TIPS

How do I adjust the volume?

To turn the volume up or down, click and drag the **Volume** slider to the left (to reduce the volume) or to the right (to increase the volume). You can also press ⌘+⬇ to reduce the volume, or ⌘+⬆ to increase the volume.

Can I share my music with my family?

Yes, you can activate Home Sharing, which enables you to share your iTunes library with other people on your network as long as you are all logged in to Home Sharing with the same Apple ID. Click **File**, click **Home Sharing**, and then click **Turn On Home Sharing**. Type your Apple password and click **Turn On Home Sharing**.

Create a Playlist

A *playlist* is a collection of songs that are related in some way. Using your iTunes library, you can create customized playlists that include only the songs that you want to hear. For example, you might want to create a playlist of upbeat or festive songs to play during a party or celebration. Similarly, you might want to create a playlist of your current favorite songs to burn to a CD. Whatever the reason, once you create the playlist you can populate it with songs using a simple drag-and-drop technique.

Create a Playlist

Create the Playlist

1 Click **File**.

2 Click **New**.

3 Click **Playlist**.

Note: You can also create a new playlist by pressing ⌘+N.

A iTunes creates a new playlist.

4 Type a name for the new playlist.

5 Press Return.

6 Click **Edit Playlist**.

iTunes opens the playlist for editing so that you can add your songs.

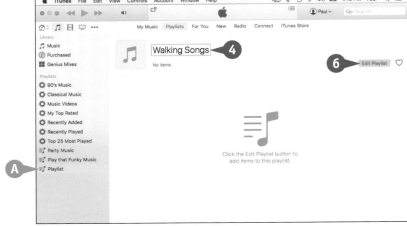

Add Songs to the Playlist

1 Open an album that has one or more songs you want to add to the playlist.

2 Click a song that you want to add to the playlist.

Note: If you want more than one song from the album's playlist, press and hold ⌘ and click each of the songs you want to add.

3 Drag the selected track and drop it on your playlist.

4 Repeat steps **2** and **3** to add more songs to the playlist.

5 Click **Done**.

B To access your playlists, click **Playlists**.

TIPS

Is there a faster way to create and populate a playlist?
Yes. Press and hold ⌘ and then click each song you want to include in your playlist. Click **File**, click **New**, and then click **Playlist from Selection** (you can also press Shift+⌘+N). Type the playlist name and then press Return.

Can iTunes add songs to a playlist automatically?
Yes, you can create a *Smart Playlist* where the songs have one or more properties in common, such as the genre or text in the song title. Click **File**, click **New**, and then click **Smart Playlist** (you can also press Option+⌘+N). Use the Smart Playlist dialog to create rules that define what songs appear in the playlist.

Purchase Music from the iTunes Store

You can add music to your iTunes library by purchasing songs or albums from the iTunes Store. iTunes downloads the song or album to your computer and then adds it to both the Music category and the Purchased playlist. You can then play and manage the song or album just like any other content in the iTunes library. To purchase music from the iTunes Store, you must have an Apple ID, which you can obtain from https://appleid.apple.com.

Purchase Music from the iTunes Store

1 Click **iTunes Store**.

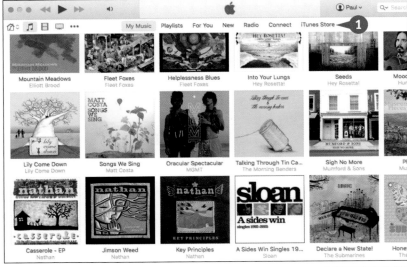

The iTunes Store appears.

2 Click **Music**.

3 Locate the music you want to purchase.

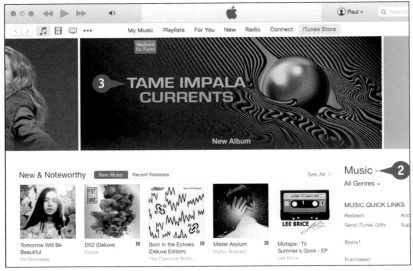

Ⓐ You can use the Search box to search for an artist, album, or song.

④ Click **Buy**.

Ⓑ If you want to purchase just a song, click the song's price button instead.

iTunes asks you to sign in to your iTunes Store account.

⑤ If you have not signed in to your account, you must type your Apple ID.

⑥ Type your password.

⑦ Click **Buy**.

iTunes charges your credit card and begins downloading the music to your Mac.

Ⓒ To return to the iTunes library, click **My Music**.

TIPS

Can I use my purchased music on other computers and devices?

Yes. When you purchase music through iTunes, you are given a license to play that music on any device (such as an iPod, iPad, or iPhone), as long as that device is signed in to iCloud using the same Apple ID that you used to purchase the music. You can also burn your music to CDs.

How do I redeem an iTunes gift card?

Scratch off the sticker that covers the card's redeem code. Access the iTunes Store, click **Redeem**, and then enter your account password. In the Redeem Code screen, type the redemption code and then click **Redeem**.

Apply Parental Controls

If you are setting up a user account in Mac Pro for a child, you can use iTunes' parental controls to ensure the child does not have access to music that has been marked as having explicit content. You can also disable certain content types — such as podcasts, the iTunes Store, and Internet radio stations — that could potentially offer content not suitable for the child. Finally, you can also disable access to shared iTunes libraries, which might contain unsuitable music.

Apply Parental Controls

1 Log in to OS X using the child's user account.

2 Click **iTunes**.

3 Click **Preferences**.

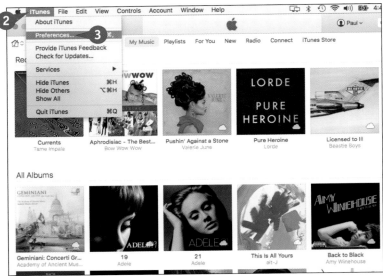

The iTunes preferences appear.

4 Click the **Parental** tab.

5 In the Disable section, click the check box beside each type of content you do not want the user to access (☐ changes to ✓).

6 Click the **Ratings for** ⬦ and then click the country ratings you want to use.

7 To ensure the user cannot access explicit musical content, click the **Music with explicit content** check box (☐ changes to ✓).

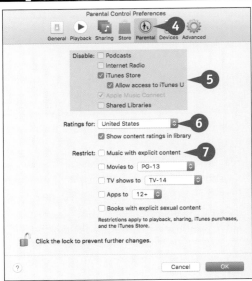

iTunes displays an overview of what it means to restrict explicit content.

⑧ Click **OK**.

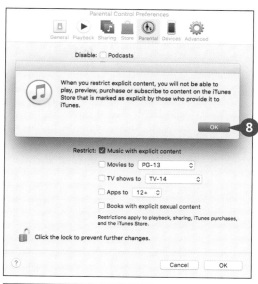

⑨ Click **OK**.

iTunes puts the parental controls into effect.

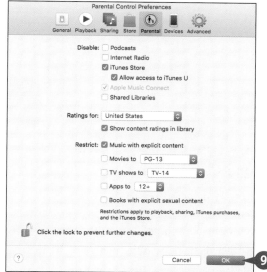

Is it not possible for the child to open the iTunes preferences and disable the parent controls?
Yes, although this is not likely to be a concern for young children. However, for older children who know their way around OS X, you should lock the parental controls to avoid having them changed. Follow steps 1 to 4 to open the child's user account and display the Parental tab. Click the lock icon (🔓), type your OS X administrator password, and then click **OK**. 🔓 changes to 🔒, indicating that the controls in the Parental tab are now locked and can be unlocked only with your administrator password. Click **OK**.

Subscribe to a Podcast

You can use iTunes to locate, subscribe, manage, and listen to your favorite podcasts. A *podcast* is an audio feed — or sometimes a feed that combines both audio and video — that a publisher updates regularly with new episodes. The easiest way to get each episode is to subscribe to the podcast. This ensures that iTunes automatically downloads each new episode to your iTunes library. You can subscribe to podcasts via either the publisher's website or the iTunes Store.

Subscribe to a Podcast

1 Click **iTunes Store**.

2 Click **Podcasts**.

3 Locate the podcast to which you want to subscribe.

4 Click **Subscribe**.

A If you want to listen to just one episode before subscribing, click the episode's **Get** button instead.

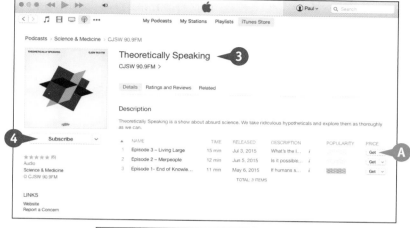

iTunes asks you to confirm.

5 Click **Subscribe**.

iTunes begins downloading the podcast.

To listen to the podcast, click the subscription in the Podcasts category of the library.

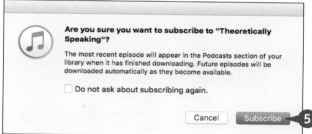

TIP

How do I subscribe to a podcast via the web?

Use your web browser to navigate to the podcast's home page, click the **iTunes** link to open a preview of the podcast, click **View in iTunes**, and then follow steps 4 and 5.

If the podcast does not have an iTunes link, copy the address of the podcast feed, switch to iTunes, click **File**, and then click **Subscribe to Podcast**. In the Subscribe to Podcast dialog, paste the address of the podcast feed into the URL text box and then click **OK**.

CHAPTER 8

Learning Useful OS X Tasks

OS X El Capitan comes with many tools that help you accomplish everyday tasks. In this chapter, you learn how to synchronize an iPod, iPhone, or iPad; work with notes and reminders; post to Facebook or Twitter; share data; and work with notifications, tags, and maps.

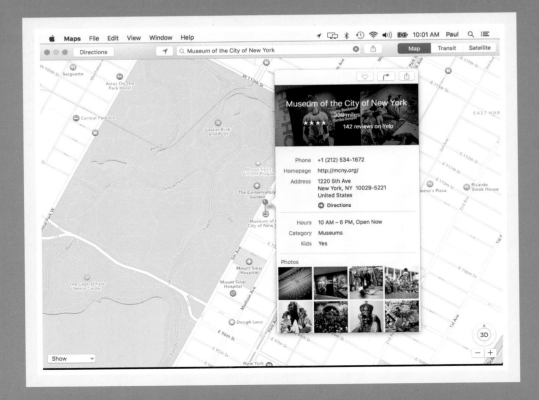

Connect an iPhone, iPad, or iPod touch

To synchronize some or all of your iTunes library — including music, podcasts, audiobooks, TV shows, and movies — as well as your photos and e-books, with your iPhone, iPad, or iPod touch, you can connect the device to your Mac.

Although you can synchronize over Wi-Fi, if your device is not running a recent version of iOS, or if your Mac and your device are not on the same network, you must physically connect your device to your Mac. You need the USB cable that came with the device package. You can also connect using an optional dock.

Connect an iPhone, iPad, or iPod touch

Connect the Device Directly

1 Attach the USB cable's Lightning connector to the device's port.

2 Attach the cable's USB connector to a free USB port on your Mac.

3 If your device asks if you trust this computer, tap **Trust** on the device and click **Continue** on your Mac.

OS X launches iTunes and automatically begins synchronizing the device.

Connect the Device Using the Dock

1 Attach the USB cable's Lightning connector to the dock's port.

2 Insert the device into the dock.

3 Attach the cable's USB connector to a free USB port on your Mac.

4 If your device asks if you trust this computer, tap **Trust** on the device and click **Continue** on your Mac.

OS X launches iTunes and automatically begins synchronizing the device.

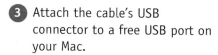

TIP

Do I have to eject my device before disconnecting it?
No, you can disconnect the device at any time as long as no sync is in progress. If a sync is in progress and you need to disconnect, first click **Cancel Sync** (✖) in the iTunes status window, wait until the sync is canceled, and then disconnect your device.

Synchronize an iPod, iPhone, or iPad

You can take your media and other data with you by synchronizing that data from OS X to your iPod touch, iPhone, or iPad. However, you should synchronize movies and TV shows with care. A single half-hour TV episode may be as large as 650MB, and full-length movies can be several gigabytes. To synchronize your device, first connect it to your Mac.

Synchronize an iPod, iPhone, or iPad

Synchronize Music

1. Click your device's icon.

2. Click **Music**.

3. Click **Sync Music** (☐ changes to ✅).

4. Click **Selected playlists, artists, albums, and genres** (◯ changes to ◉).

5. Click each item you want to synchronize (☐ changes to ✅).

6. Click **Apply**.

   iTunes synchronizes your music.

7. If you have finished syncing your device, click **Music** (♫).

Synchronize Photos

1. Click your device's icon.

2. Click **Photos**.

3. Click **Sync Photos** (☐ changes to ✅).

4. Click **Selected albums, Events, and Faces, and automatically include** (◯ changes to ◉).

5. Click each item you want to synchronize (☐ changes to ✅).

6. Click **Apply**.

   iTunes synchronizes your photos.

7. If you have finished syncing your device, click **Music** (♫).

Synchronize Movies

1. Click the icon for your device.

2. Click **Movies**.

3. Click **Sync Movies** (☐ changes to ✓).

4. Click each movie you want to synchronize (☐ changes to ✓).

5. Click **Apply**.

   iTunes synchronizes your movies.

6. If you have finished syncing your device, click **Music** (♫).

Synchronize TV Shows

1. Click the icon for your device.

2. Click **TV Shows**.

3. Click **Sync TV Shows** (☐ changes to ✓).

4. Click each TV show you want to synchronize (☐ changes to ✓).

5. Click **Apply**.

   iTunes synchronizes your TV shows.

6. If you have finished syncing your device, click **Music** (♫).

TIPS

Can I sync wirelessly?
Yes. Connect your device and select it in iTunes, click the **Summary** tab, and then click **Sync with this** *device* **over Wi-Fi**, where *device* is an iPhone, iPad, or iPod (☐ changes to ✓). To sync over Wi-Fi, on your device tap **Settings**, tap **General**, tap **iTunes Wi-Fi Sync**, and then tap **Sync Now**.

How do I get my photos from my device to my Mac?
You can view and work with device pictures on your Mac by importing them into iPhoto. In iPhoto, click your device and then press and hold ⌘ and click each photo you want to import. Use the Event Name text box to type a name for this event and then click **Import Selected**.

Integrate OS X and Your iPhone or iPad

Continuity is a set of features that enable you to integrate your Mac and your iPhone or iPad (as well as your iPod touch). Continuity consists of three features: Handoff, for continuing tasks on one device that you started on another; taking phone calls on your Mac or sending Mac calls to your iPhone; and Personal Hotspot for sharing your device's Internet connection with your Mac.

For the Continuity features to work, your Mac must be running OS X Yosemite or later and your iPhone or iPad must be running iOS 8 or later. Also, your Mac and your device must be signed in to the same iCloud account.

Handoff

The Handoff feature enables you to begin certain tasks on your iPhone or iPad and then continue those tasks on your Mac. Handoff-compatible tasks include composing an email, writing a text message, browsing a web page, and working with apps such as Maps, Reminders, Calendar, and Contacts. Handoff works both ways, so if you start a task on your Mac, you can continue it on your iPhone or iPad.

Phone Calls

Continuity enables you to initiate iPhone calls from your Mac. For example, if you come across a phone number while using Safari on your Mac, select the number, click the arrow that appears, and then click **Call "*Number*" Using iPhone** (where *Number* is the selected phone number). You can also initiate calls from Contacts or Calendar.

If your iPhone receives an incoming call, your Mac displays a notification that you can click to answer the call on your Mac.

Personal Hotspot

If your Mac cannot connect to a Wi-Fi network for Internet access, you can still get your Mac online by using your iPhone's (or iPad's) cellular connection as a temporary wireless network. When you enable the device's Personal Hotspot (tap **Settings** and then **Personal Hotspot**), your device appears in your Mac's list of nearby Wi-Fi networks. Select the device and type the password to connect.

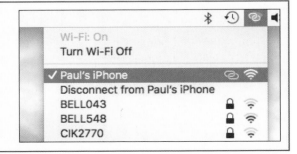

Enable Handoff in OS X

The Handoff feature enables you to use OS X to continue a task begun on your iPhone or iPad. Handoff requires that your iPhone or iPad is running iOS 8 or later, is close to your Mac (within about 30 feet), and has Bluetooth activated. Also, your Mac must be running OS X Yosemite or later, it must be relatively new (two or three years old at most), and it must have Bluetooth activated. Finally, as shown in this section, you must configure OS X to accept Handoff connections between your device and your Mac.

Enable Handoff in OS X

1 Click **Apple** ().

2 Click **System Preferences**.

3 Click **General**.

The General preferences appear.

4 Click the **Allow Handoff between this Mac and your iCloud devices** check box (changes to).

5 Click **Close** ().

OS X now accepts Handoff connections between your Mac and your iPhone or iPad.

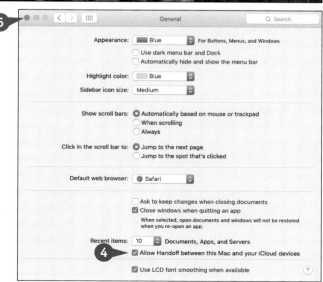

Install a Program Using the App Store

You can enhance and extend OS X by installing new programs from the App Store. OS X comes with an impressive collection of applications — or *apps*. However, OS X does not offer a complete collection of apps. For example, OS X lacks apps in categories such as productivity, personal finance, and business tools. To fill in these gaps, you can use the App Store to locate, purchase, and install new programs, or look for apps that go beyond what the default OS X programs can do.

Install a Program Using the App Store

1 In the Dock, click **App Store** (▲).

The App Store window appears.

2 Locate the app you want to install.

3 Click the price button or, if the app is free, as shown here, click the **Get** button instead.

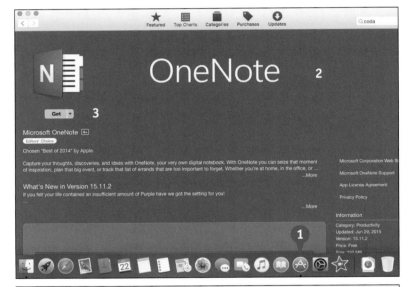

The price button changes to a Buy App button, or the Free button changes to an Install App button.

4 Click **Buy App** (or **Install App**).

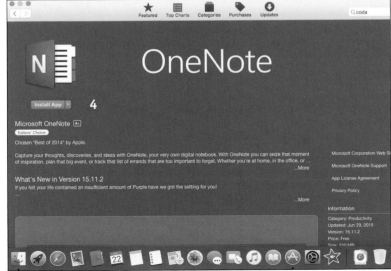

The App Store prompts you to log in with your Apple ID.

⑤ Type your Apple ID.

⑥ Type your password.

⑦ Click **Sign In**.

Ⓐ The App Store begins downloading the app.

When the progress meter disappears, your app is installed. Click **Launchpad** (🚀) and then click the app to run it.

TIP

How do I use an App Store gift card to purchase apps?
If you have an App Store or iTunes gift card, you can redeem the card to give yourself store credit in the amount shown on the card. Scratch off the sticker on the back to reveal the code. Click **App Store** (Ⓐ) to open the App Store, click **Featured**, click **Redeem**, type the code, and then click **Redeem**. In the App Store window, the Account item shows your current store credit balance. Be sure to redeem the card before you make a purchase; you cannot apply the credit after the purchase is made.

Write a Note

You can use the Notes app to create simple text documents for things such as to-do lists and meeting notes. Word processing programs such as Word and Pages are useful for creating complex and lengthy documents. However, these powerful tools feel like overkill when all you want to do is jot down a few notes. For these simpler text tasks, the Notes app that comes with OS X is perfect because it offers a simple interface that keeps all your notes together. As you see in the next section, you can also pin a note to the OS X desktop for easy access.

Write a Note

Create a New Note

1 In the Dock, click **Notes** ( ).

The first time you start Notes, it displays an overview of the app.

2 Click **Continue**.

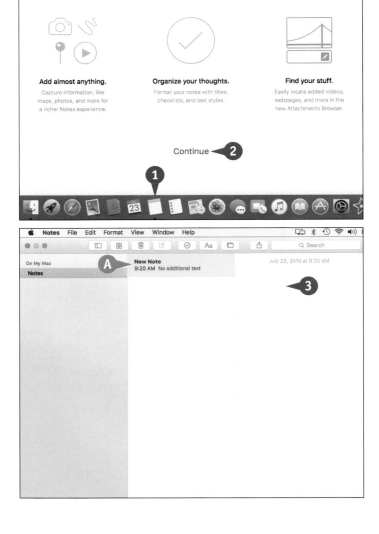

The Notes window appears.

Ⓐ When you first start Notes, the app creates a new note for you automatically.

3 Click inside the note pane.

④ Type your note text.

Ⓑ Notes uses the first line as the note title.

⑤ To create another note, click **New Note** (✑).

Note: You can also click **File** and then click **New Note**, or press ⌘+Ⓝ.

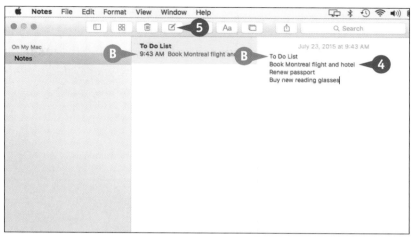

Delete a Note

① Click the note you want to delete.

② Click **Delete** (🗑).

The Notes app deletes the note.

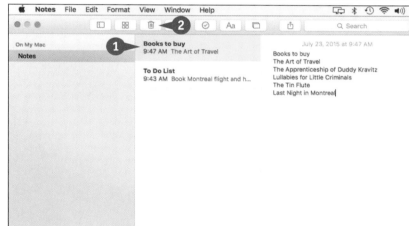

TIPS

Can I synchronize my notes with my iPhone or iPad?
Yes, as long as you have an iCloud account set up in OS X, as described in Chapter 14, and you are syncing notes between your Mac and iCloud. To create a new note using iCloud, click **Notes** under the iCloud folder and then follow the steps in this section.

Can I create a bulleted or numbered list?
No, but you can create a checklist, which is a list of items with check boxes to the left of each item. When an item is complete, click its check box (☐ changes to ✅). To create a checklist, click **Format**, and then click **Checklist**.

Enhance Notes with Attachments

You can enhance your notes by adding links to websites and by attaching files such as photos and documents. Most of your notes will contain only text, but you might need to augment a note with extra data, such as a link to a website that contains related content. Similarly, you can enhance your notes with related files such as photos, videos, maps, audio files, and documents.

Besides enhancing existing notes, you can also create notes that consist only of external links and files. For example, you could create a note that has links to websites on a particular topic.

Enhance Notes with Attachments

Add an Attachment to a Note

1. Open the application that contains the item you want to attach.

2. Select or display the item, such as a web page, as in this example.

3. Click **Share** (⬆).

4. Click **Notes**.

The Notes dialog appears.

Ⓐ The item appears in the note.

⑤ Type an optional description of the item.

⑥ Click the **Choose Note** ↕ and then click the note to which you want to attach the item.

Note: To attach the item to a new note, click **New Note** in the Choose Note list.

⑦ Click **Save**.

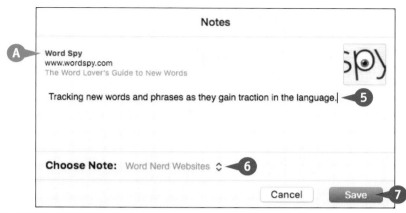

View Note Attachments

① In the Notes app, click **Browse attachments** (⊞).

Notes displays the Attachment Browser.

② Click an attachment category.

Ⓑ Notes displays the items in the category from all your notes.

③ Click **Browse attachments** (⊞) to return to your notes.

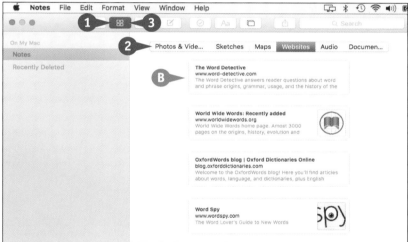

I have a lot of notes. Is there an easy way to see the note to which an item is attached?

Yes. Follow steps **1** and **2** in the subsection "View Note Attachments" to display the category of the attachment you want to view. Right-click the attachment and then click **Go to Note**. Notes exits the Attachment Browser and displays the note that contains the attachment.

How do I open an attachment in its original application?

Follow steps **1** and **2** in the subsection "View Note Attachments" to display the category of the attachment you want to open. Right-click the attachment and then click **Open Attachment** (you can also double-click the attachment).

Create a Reminder

You can use Reminders to have OS X display a notification when you need to perform a task. You can use Calendar to schedule important events, but you likely have many tasks during the day that cannot be considered full-fledged events: returning a call, taking clothes out of the dryer, turning off the sprinkler. If you need to be reminded to perform such tasks, Calendar is overkill, but OS X offers a better solution: Reminders. You use this app to create reminders, which are notifications that tell you to do something or to be somewhere.

Create a Reminder

1 In the Dock, click **Reminders** (▦).

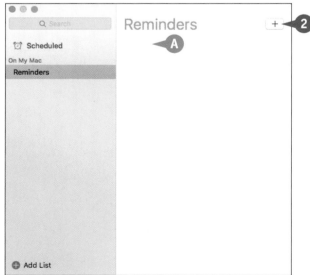

The Reminders app appears.

2 Click **New Reminder** (+).

Ⓐ You can also click the next available line in the Reminders list.

Note: You can also click **File** and then click **New Reminder**, or press ⌘+N.

3 Type the reminder title.

4 Click **Show Info** (ⓘ).

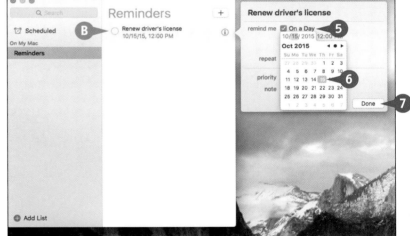

The Reminders app displays the reminder details.

5 Click the **On a Day** check box (☐ changes to ✓).

6 Specify the date and time you want to be reminded.

7 Click **Done**.

The Reminders app adds the reminder to the list.

B When you have completed the reminder, click its radio button (◯ changes to ◉).

TIP

What does the At a Location option do?

The At a Location option allows the Reminders app to display a notification for a task when you arrive at or leave a location and you have your Mac notebook with you. To set this up, follow steps **1** to **4**, click the **At a Location** check box (☐ changes to ✓), and then type the address or choose a contact that has a defined address. Click either the **Leaving** or the **Arriving** option (◯ changes to ◉) and then click **Done**.

Create a New Reminder List

You can organize your reminders and make them easier to locate by creating new reminder lists. By default, Reminders comes with a single list called Reminders. However, if you use reminders frequently, the Reminders list can become cluttered, making it difficult to locate reminders. To solve this problem, you can organize your reminders by creating new lists. For example, you could have one list for personal tasks and another for business tasks. After you create one or more new lists, you can move some or all of your existing reminders to the appropriate lists.

Create a New Reminder List

Create a Reminder List

1 Click **Add List**.

Note: You can also click **File** and then click **New List**, or press ⌘+L.

A The Reminders app adds the new list to the sidebar.

2 Type the list name.

3 Press **Return**.

Move a Reminder to a Different List

1 Click the list that contains the reminder you want to move.

2 Click and drag the reminder and drop it on the destination list.

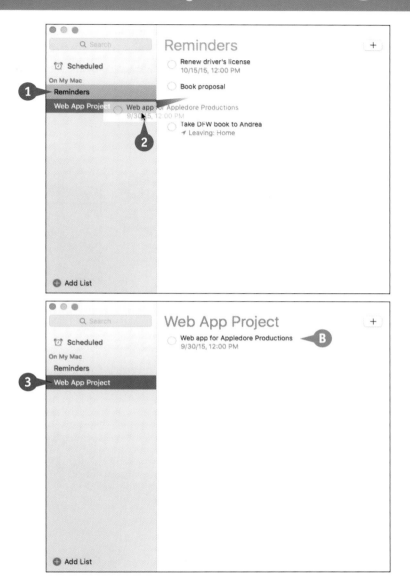

3 Click the destination list.

B The reminder now appears in the destination list.

Note: You can also right-click the reminder, click **Move to List**, and then click the destination list.

TIPS

Why does my Reminders app not have a Completed list?

The Reminders app does not show the Completed list when you first start using the program. When you mark a reminder as complete (○ changes to ◉), Reminders creates the Completed list and moves the task to that list.

Can I change the order of the lists in the sidebar?

Yes. By default, the Reminders app displays the new lists in the order you create them. To move a list to a new position, click and drag the list up or down in the sidebar. When the horizontal blue bar shows the list to be in the position you want, release the mouse button.

Work with the Notification Center

You can keep on top of what is happening while you are using your Mac by taking advantage of the Notification Center. Several apps take advantage of a feature called *notifications,* which enables them to send messages to OS X about events that are happening on your Mac. For example, the App Store uses the Notification Center to let you know when OS X updates are available. There are two types of notifications: a banner that appears temporarily and an alert that stays on-screen until you dismiss it. You can also open the Notification Center to view recent notifications.

Work with the Notification Center

Handle Alert Notifications

A An alert notification displays one or more buttons.

1 Click a button to dismiss the notification.

Note: In a notification about new OS X updates, click **Update** to open the App Store and see the updates. For details about the updates, click **Details**.

Handle Banner Notifications

B A banner notification does not display any buttons.

Note: The banner notification stays on-screen for about 5 seconds and then disappears.

View Recent Notifications

1 Click **Notification Center** (☰).

Note: If your Mac has a trackpad, you can also open the Notification Center by using two fingers to swipe left from the right edge of the trackpad.

2 Click **Notifications**.

C OS X displays your recent notifications.

3 Click a notification to view the item in the original application.

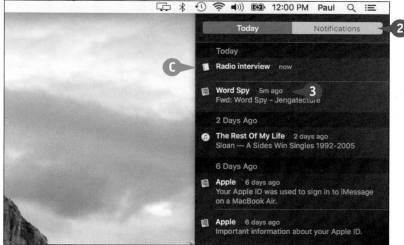

TIP

Can I control which apps use the Notification Center and how they use it?
Yes. Click **System Preferences** (⚙) in the Dock and then click **Notifications**. Click an app on the left side of the window and then click a notification style: None, Banners, or Alerts. To control the number of items the app can display in the Notification Center, click the **Show in Notification Center** option menu and select a number. To remove an app from the Notification Center, click the **Show in Notification Center** check box (☑ changes to ☐).

Organize Files with Tags

You can describe many of your files to OS X by adding one or more tags that indicate the content or subject matter of the file. A *tag* is a word or short phrase that describes some aspect of a file. You can add as many tags as you need. Adding tags to files makes it easier to search and organize your documents.

For an existing file, you can add one or more tags within Finder. If you are working with a new file, you can add tags when you save the file to your Mac's hard drive.

Organize Files with Tags

Add Tags with Finder

1 Click **Finder** ( ) in the Dock.

2 Open the folder that contains the file you want to tag.

3 Click the file.

4 Click **Edit Tags** ( ).

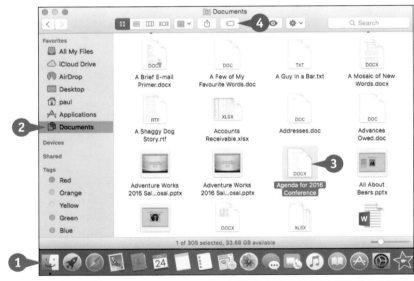

OS X displays the Tags sheet.

5 Type the tag.

Note: To assign multiple tags, separate each one with a comma.

6 Press Return.

OS X assigns the tag or tags.

7 Press Return.

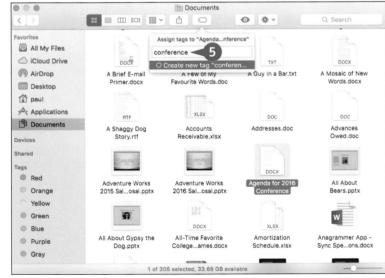

Add Tags When Saving

① In the application, select the command that saves the new file.

The application displays the Save sheet.

② Use the Tags text box to type the tag.

Note: To assign multiple tags, separate each one with a comma.

③ Choose the other save options, such as the file name, as needed.

④ Click **Save**.

The application saves the file and assigns that tag or tags.

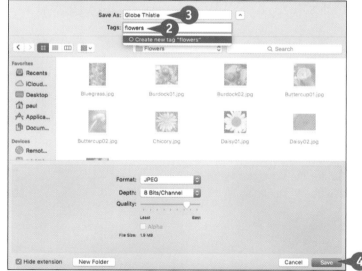

TIPS

Is there an easier method I can use to assign an existing tag to another file?

Yes. OS X keeps a list of your tags, and it displays that list each time you display the Tags sheet. You can assign the same tag to another file by displaying the Tags sheet and clicking the tag in the list that appears.

Can I assign the same tag or tags to multiple files?

Yes. First, use Finder to select all the files in advance. Click **Edit Tags** (⬭), type the tag, and OS X automatically assigns the tag to all the selected files.

Search Files with Tags

After you assign tags to your files, you can take advantage of those tags to make it easier to find and group related files.

Although keeping related files together in the same folder is good practice, that is not always possible. It can make locating and working with related files difficult. However, if you assign the same tag or tags to those files, you can use those tags to quickly and easily search for the files. No matter where the files are located, Finder shows them all together in a single window for easy access.

Search Files with Tags

Search for a Tag

1 Type the first few letters of the tag in Finder's Search box.

2 When the tag appears, click it.

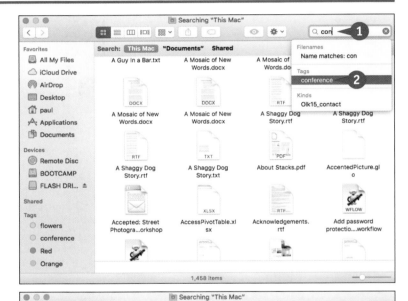

A Finder displays the files assigned that tag.

Select a Tag

1 In the Finder sidebar, click the tag.

B If you do not see the tag you want, click **All Tags** to display the complete list.

C Finder displays the files assigned that tag.

Note: With the tag folder displayed, you can automatically assign that tag to other files by dragging the files from another Finder window and dropping them within the tag folder.

TIP

Can I control what tags appear in Finder's sidebar?
Yes, by following these steps:

1 Open Finder.

2 Click **Finder**.

3 Click **Preferences**.

4 Click the **Tags** tab.

5 For each tag you do not want to appear in the sidebar, click the check box to the right of the tag (☑ changes to ☐).

6 Click **Close** (●).

Search for a Location

You can use the Maps app to display a location on a map. Maps is an OS X app that displays digital maps that you can use to view just about any location by searching for an address or place name.

Maps comes with a Search box that enables you to search for locations by address or by name. If Maps finds the place, it zooms in and drops a pin on the digital map to show you the exact location. For many public locations, Maps also offers an info screen that shows you the location's address, phone number, and more.

Search for a Location

1. Click **Maps** (⬚).

   The first time you start Maps, OS X asks if the app can use your location.

2. Click **Allow**.

   OS X starts the Maps app.

3. Use the Search box to type the address or name of the location.

4. Press **Return**.

   Ⓐ If Maps displays the name of the location as you type, you can click the location, instead.

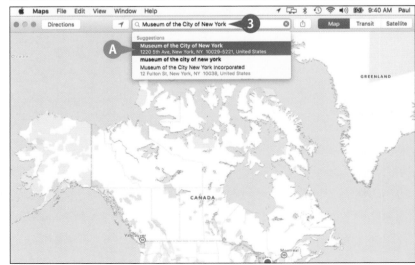

Ⓑ Maps drops a pin on the location.

Ⓒ Click **Zoom In** (+) or press ⌘+⊕ to get a closer look.

Ⓓ Click **Zoom Out** (—) or press ⌘+⊖ to see more of the map.

⑤ If Maps offers more data about the location, click **Show Info** (ⓘ).

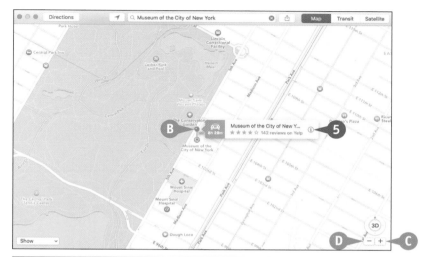

Ⓔ Maps displays the Info screen for the location.

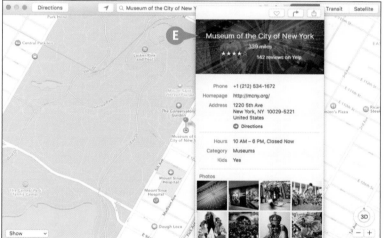

<hr />

TIPS

Can I use Maps to show my current location?
Yes. Maps can use surrounding electronic infrastructure, particularly nearby wireless networks, to come up with a reasonably accurate calculation of your current location. Click **Current Location** (➤), or click **View** and then click **Go to Current Location** (or press ⌘+L).

How do I save a location for future use?
You can save it as a favorite, which means you do not have to type the location's address or name each time. Display the location, click **Show Info** (ⓘ), click **Share** (⬆), and then click **Add to Favorites**. You can also click **Edit** and then click **Add to Favorites** (or press ⌘+D).

Get Directions to a Location

esides displaying locations, Maps also understands the roads and highways found in most cities, states, and countries. This means that you can use the Maps app to get specific directions for traveling from one location to another. You specify a starting point and destination for a trip, and Maps then provides you with directions for getting from one point to the other. Maps highlights the trip route on a digital map and also gives you specific details for negotiating each leg of the trip.

Get Directions to a Location

1 Add a pin to the map for your destination.

Note: See the previous section, "Search for a Location," to learn how to add a pin.

2 Click **Directions**.

The Directions pane appears.

Ⓐ Your pinned location appears in the End text box.

Maps assumes you want to start the route from your current location.

3 To start the route from another location, type the name or address in the Start text box.

4 Select how you intend to travel to the destination: Drive, Walk, or take Transit.

B Maps displays the suggested route for your journey.

C This area tells the distance and approximate traveling time.

D This area displays the various legs of the journey.

E If Maps displays alternate routes, you can click these banners to view the routes.

5 Click the first leg of the trip.

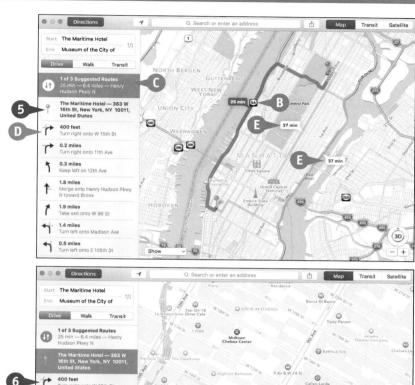

F Maps zooms in to show you just that leg of the trip.

6 As you complete each leg of the trip, click the next leg for further instructions.

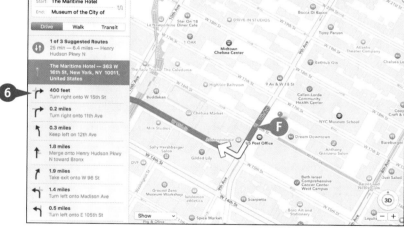

TIPS

Can I get traffic information?
Yes, Maps can display current traffic conditions for most major cities. Click **View** and then click **Show Traffic**. On the map, you see a sequence of red dots where traffic is slow, and a sequence of red dashes where traffic is heavy.

Can I get directions even though I do not have an exact address?
Yes. You can give Maps the approximate location and it generates the appropriate directions. To specify a location without knowing its address, click **Edit** and then click **Drop Pin** (or press Shift+⌘+D). Maps drops a purple pin randomly on the map. Click and drag the pin to the location you want.

Install a Font

OS X ships with a large collection of fonts, but if you require a different font for a project, you can download the font files and then install them on your Mac.

Macs have always placed special emphasis on typography, so it is no surprise that OS X ships with nearly 300 fonts. However, typography is a personal, exacting art form, so your Mac might not have a particular font that would be just right for a newsletter, greeting card, or similar project. In that case, you can download the font you need and then install it.

Install a Font

1 Click **Finder** (   ).

   The Finder window appears.

2 Open the folder that contains the font files.

3 Select the font files you want to install.

4 Click **File**.

5 Click **Open**.

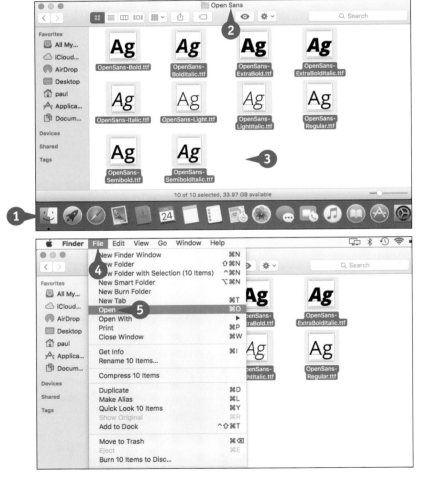

OS X launches the Font Book application.

6 Click **Install Font**.

Font Book installs the font.

A The typeface name appears in the Fonts list.

7 Click ▶ to open the typeface and see its individual fonts.

8 Click a font.

B A preview of the font appears here.

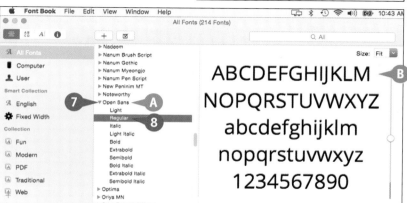

TIPS

What is the difference between a font and a typeface?

A *typeface* is a unique design applied to each letter, number, and symbol. A *font* is a particular style of a typeface, such as regular, bold, or italic. However, in everyday parlance, most people use the terms *typeface* and *font* interchangeably.

What is a font collection?

A *collection* is a group of related fonts. For example, the Fun collection contains fonts normally used with informal designs. To add your font to an existing collection, drag it from the **Fonts** list and drop it on the collection. To create a collection, click **File** and then click **New Collection** (or press ⌘+N).

Access Non-Keyboard Characters

You can make your documents more readable and more useful by inserting special symbols not available via your keyboard. The keyboard is home to a large number of letters, numbers, and symbols. However, the keyboard is missing some useful characters. For example, it is missing the foreign characters in words such as café and Köln. Similarly, your writing might require mathematical symbols such as ÷ and ½, financial symbols such as ¢ and ¥, or commercial symbols such as © and ®. These and many more symbols and emoji icons are available in OS X via the Emoji & Symbols Viewer.

Access Non-Keyboard Characters

Display the Character Viewer

1. Click **System Preferences** (⚙).

   The System Preferences appear.

2. Click **Keyboard**.

The Keyboard preferences appear.

3. Click the **Keyboard** tab.

4. Click the **Show Keyboard, Emoji, & Symbol Viewers in menu bar** check box (☐ changes to ☑).

5. Click **Keyboard, Emoji, & Symbol Viewers** (▦).

6. Click **Show Emoji & Symbols**.

   The Emoji & Symbols viewer appears.

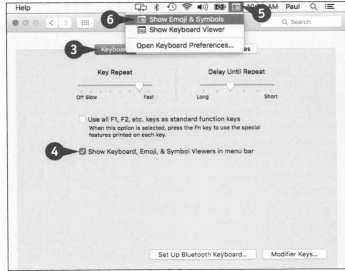

Insert a Character

1 In the document, position the insertion point where you want the character to appear.

2 In the Emoji & Symbols viewer, select a category.

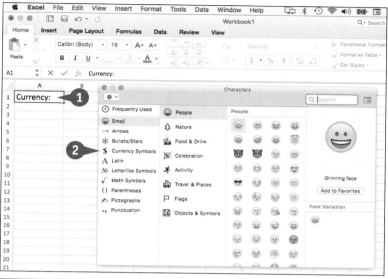

3 Double-click the character you want to use.

A The character appears in the document at the insertion point.

4 Click **Close** (●).

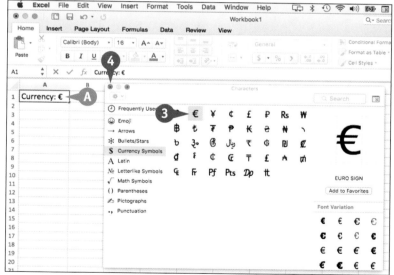

TIPS

Can I access the Character Viewer if I choose not to display the menu bar icon?

Yes, in some applications you can access the Emoji & Symbols viewer directly. For example, in TextEdit, you can click **Edit** and then click **Emoji & Symbols**, or you can press Control + ⌘ + Spacebar. This command is also available in Calendar, Contacts, Mail, Messages, and Notes.

Is there an easier way to access characters that I often use?

Yes, you can add those characters to Emoji & Symbol viewer's Favorites section. To add a character to the Favorites section, display the Emoji & Symbols viewer, click the character, and then click **Add to Favorites**.

CHAPTER 9

Connecting to Social Networks

In this age of ubiquitous social connection, OS X makes everything easier by enabling you to connect and post content to a number of social networks, including Facebook, Twitter, LinkedIn, Flickr, and Vimeo.

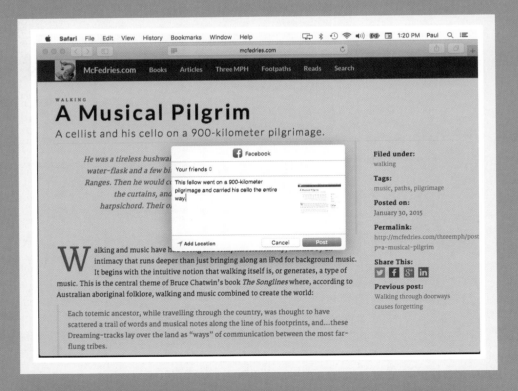

Sign In to Your Facebook Account

If you have a Facebook account, you can use it to share information with your friends directly from OS X because OS X has built-in support for Facebook accounts. This enables you to post status updates and other data directly from many OS X apps. For example, you can send a link to a web page from Safari or post a photo from Photos. OS X also displays notifications when your Facebook friends post to your News Feed. Before you can post or see Facebook notifications, you must sign in to your Facebook account.

Sign In to Your Facebook Account

① Click **System Preferences** (⚙).

Note: You can also click **Apple** (🍎) and then click **System Preferences**.

The System Preferences appear.

② Click **Internet Accounts**.

The Internet Accounts preferences appear.

③ Click **Facebook**.

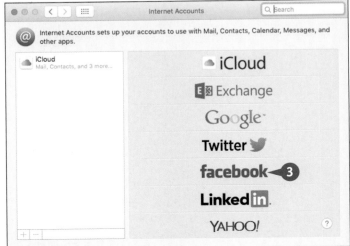

System Preferences prompts you for your Facebook username and password.

④ Type your Facebook username.

⑤ Type your Facebook password.

⑥ Click **Next**.

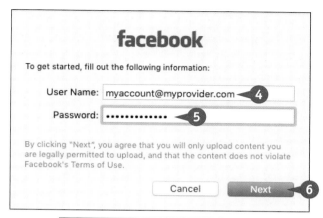

System Preferences displays information detailing what signing in to Facebook entails.

⑦ Click **Sign In**.

OS X signs in to your Facebook account.

TIPS

Is there an easy way to add my Facebook friends' profile pictures to the Contacts app?

Yes. Follow steps **1** and **2** to open the Internet Accounts window, click your Facebook account, and then click **Update Contacts**. When System Preferences asks you to confirm, click **Update Contacts**.

Can I prevent Facebook friends and events from appearing in the Contacts and Calendar apps?

Yes. Follow steps **1** and **2** to open Internet Accounts and then click your Facebook account. To remove your Facebook friends from Contacts, click the **Contacts** check box (☑ changes to ☐). To remove your Facebook events or friends' birthdays from Calendar, click the **Calendars** check box (☑ changes to ☐).

Post to Facebook

Once you sign in to your Facebook account, you begin seeing notifications whenever your friends post to your News Feed. However, OS X's Facebook support also enables you to use various OS X apps to post information to your Facebook News Feed. For example, if you surf to a web page that you want to share, you can post a link to that page. You can also post a photo to your News Feed.

Post to Facebook

Post a Web Page

1. Use Safari to navigate to the web page you want to share.

2. Click **Share** (⬆).

3. Click **Facebook**.

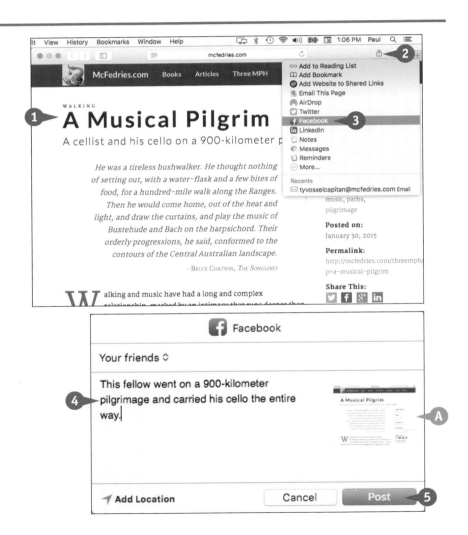

OS X displays the Facebook share sheet.

Ⓐ The web page appears as an attachment inside the post.

4. Type your post text.

5. Click **Post**.

Post a Photo

1 In Finder, open the folder that contains the photo you want to share.

2 Click the photo.

3 Click **Share** (⬆).

4 Click **Facebook**.

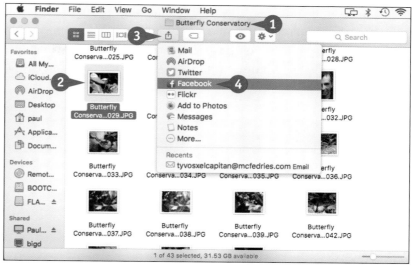

OS X displays the Facebook share sheet.

Ⓑ The photo appears as an attachment inside the post.

5 Type some text to accompany the photo.

6 Click **Post**.

TIPS

How do I control who sees the links and photos that I post to Facebook?

In the Facebook share sheet, click **Your Friends** to open a pop-up menu that lists your sharing choices, including your Facebook groups and three predefined choices: Public (anyone can view the post), Your Friends (only your Facebook friends can view the post), and Only Me (only you can view the post).

Can I add a location to my Facebook posts?

Yes, in the Facebook share sheet, click **Add Location**. Note that when you first click this link, OS X asks if Facebook is allowed to use your location, so be sure to click **Allow**.

Publish a Photos Album to Facebook

If you have connected OS X to your Facebook account, you can use that connection to publish a collection of Photos pictures to a new album in your Facebook profile. The easiest way to do this is to upload an album that you have created in Photos. However, you can also upload a selection of photos from the Photos library, or an item in the Faces or Places categories.

Publish a Photos Album to Facebook

1 In Photos, click **Albums**.

2 Click the album you want to publish to Facebook.

If you want to upload a different collection of photos, select the photos.

3 Click **Share** (⬆).

4 Click **Facebook**.

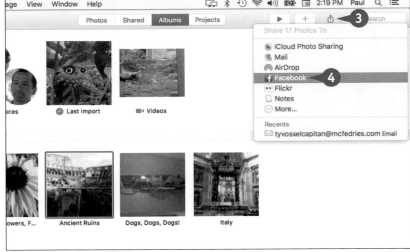

Photos displays the Facebook photo-sharing options.

5 Type a description of the photos.

6 Click **Timeline**.

Photos displays a list of your Facebook albums.

7 Click the album to which you want to add the photos.

8 Click **Post**.

TIP

Can I upload a folder of photos as a Facebook album?

No, not directly. That is, you cannot do this from Finder. Instead, you need to import the folder into Photos and then share the folder. In Photos, click **File** and then click **Import** (or press Shift+⌘+I). In the Import Photos dialog, click the folder you want to use and then click **Review for Import**. Click **Import All New Photos**. Photos imports the folder. Click **Albums**, click **Last Import**, and then share the photos to Facebook by following steps **3** to **8**.

Sign In to Your Twitter Account

If you have a Twitter account, you can use it to share information with your followers directly from OS X, which comes with built-in support for Twitter. This enables you to send tweets directly from many OS X apps. For example, you can send a link to a web page from Safari or tweet a photo from Photos. OS X also displays notifications if you are mentioned on Twitter or if a Twitter user sends you a direct message. Before you can tweet or see Twitter notifications, you must sign in to your Twitter account.

Sign In to Your Twitter Account

1 Click **System Preferences** (⊙).

Note: You can also click **Apple** () and then click **System Preferences**.

The System Preferences appear.

2 Click **Internet Accounts**.

The Internet Accounts preferences appear.

3 Click **Twitter**.

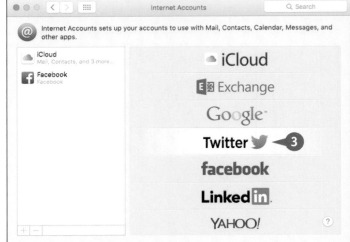

System Preferences prompts you for your Twitter username and password.

4 Type your Twitter username.

5 Type your Twitter password.

6 Click **Next**.

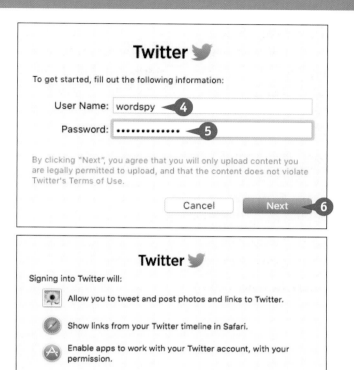

System Preferences displays information detailing what signing in to Twitter entails.

7 Click **Sign In**.

OS X signs in to your Twitter account.

TIP

Some of the people in my contacts list are on Twitter. Is there an easy way to add their Twitter usernames to the Contacts app?

Yes, OS X has a feature that enables you to give permission for Twitter to update your contacts. Twitter examines the email addresses in the Contacts app, and if it finds any that match Twitter users, it updates Contacts with each person's username and account photo.

Follow steps **1** and **2** to open the Internet Accounts window, click your Twitter account, and then click **Update Contacts**. When OS X asks you to confirm, click **Update Contacts**.

Send a Tweet

After you sign in to your Twitter account, you can send tweets from various OS X apps. Although signing in to your Twitter account is useful for seeing notifications that tell you about mentions and direct messages, you will mostly use it for sending tweets to your followers. For example, if you come across a web page that you want to share, you can tweet a link to that page. You can also take a picture using Photo Booth and tweet that picture to your followers.

Send a Tweet

Tweet a Web Page

1. Use Safari to navigate to the web page you want to share.

2. Click **Share** (⬆).

3. Click **Twitter**.

OS X displays the Tweet share sheet.

Ⓐ The attachment appears as a link inside the tweet.

4. Type your tweet text.

Ⓑ This value tells you how many characters you have remaining.

5. Click **Post**.

Tweet a Photo Booth Photo

1 Use Photo Booth to take a picture.

2 Click the picture you want to share.

3 Click **Share** (⬆).

4 Click **Twitter**.

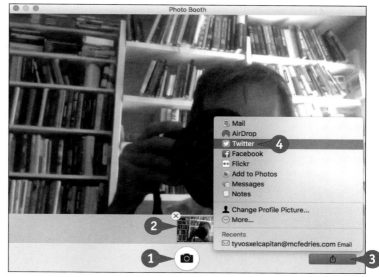

OS X displays the Twitter share sheet.

C The attachment appears as a link inside the tweet.

5 Type your tweet text.

D This value tells you how many characters you have remaining.

6 Click **Post**.

Are there other apps I can use to send tweets?

Yes. If you open a photo using Quick Look (click the photo in Finder and then press `Spacebar`), you can click **Share** (⬆) and then click **Twitter**. Similarly, you can open a photo in Preview, click **Share** (⬆), and then click **Twitter**. Also, with your permission, many third-party apps can use your sign-in information to send tweets without requiring separate Twitter logins for each app.

Can I add a location to my tweets?

Yes, but you must enable location services on OS X, as described in Chapter 11. In the Twitter share sheet, click **Add Location** to insert your current location.

Connect to Your LinkedIn Account

You can use your LinkedIn account to share information with your connections directly from OS X, because OS X comes with built-in support for LinkedIn. This enables you to use Safari to send web page links to your connections and to display the links that your connections share. OS X also displays notifications if one of your connections endorses you or sends you a message. Before you can post updates or see LinkedIn notifications, you must sign in to your LinkedIn account.

Connect to Your LinkedIn Account

1 Click **System Preferences** (🖥).

Note: You can also click **Apple** (🍎) and then click **System Preferences**.

The System Preferences appear.

2 Click **Internet Accounts**.

The Internet Accounts preferences appear.

3 Click **LinkedIn**.

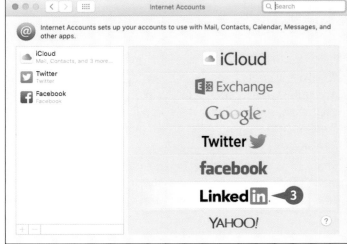

System Preferences prompts you for your LinkedIn username and password.

④ Type your LinkedIn username.

⑤ Type your LinkedIn password.

⑥ Click **Next**.

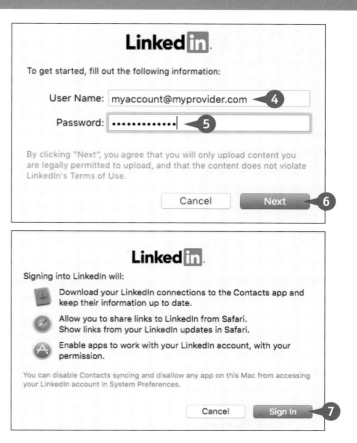

System Preferences displays information detailing what signing in to LinkedIn entails.

⑦ Click **Sign In**.

OS X signs in to your LinkedIn account.

Is there an easy way to add my LinkedIn connections' profile pictures to the Contacts app?
Yes. Follow steps **1** and **2** to open the Internet Accounts window, click your LinkedIn account, and then click **Update Contacts**. When System Preferences asks you to confirm, click **Update Contacts**.

Can I prevent my LinkedIn connections from appearing in the Contacts app?
Yes. Follow steps **1** and **2** to open the Internet Accounts window and then click your LinkedIn account. To remove your LinkedIn connections from the Contacts app, click the **Contacts** check box (✓ changes to ☐).

Post to LinkedIn

After you sign in to your LinkedIn account in OS X, you can send updates to your connections. Although signing in to your LinkedIn account is useful for seeing notifications that tell you about endorsements and other messages, you will mostly use it for sending updates to your followers. For example, if you come across a web page that you want to share, you can post a link to that page. You can share the link with just your connections or with the entire LinkedIn community.

Post to LinkedIn

1 Use Safari to navigate to the web page you want to share.

2 Click **Share** (⬆).

3 Click **LinkedIn**.

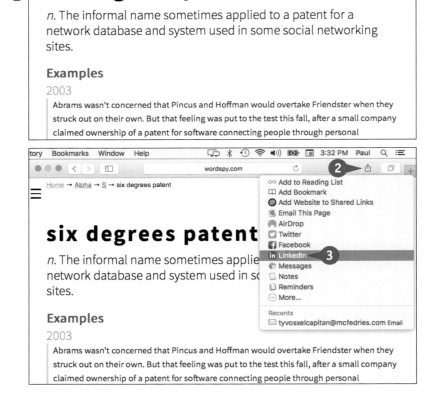

OS X displays the LinkedIn share sheet.

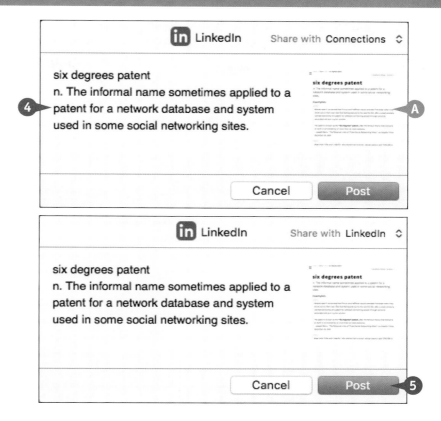

(A) The attachment appears as a link inside the post.

(4) Type your update text.

(5) Click **Post**.

OS X sends the update to LinkedIn.

How do I control who sees the updates that I post to LinkedIn?
In the LinkedIn share sheet, click the **Share with** ⬍ in the upper right corner and then click either **LinkedIn** (all of LinkedIn can view the update) or **Connections** (only your LinkedIn connections can view the post).

Are there other apps I can use to send updates?
None of the other default OS X apps support LinkedIn. However, with your permission, many third-party apps are able to use your sign-in information to send updates from the apps without requiring separate LinkedIn logins for each program.

Update Your Social Network Profile Picture

You can use OS X social network connections to easily and quickly update the profile picture for one or more of your accounts. All supported social networks identify you with a photo, which is part of your account profile. Updating this picture for just a single social network is usually a convoluted task, and it is only made worse if you want to use the same photo across multiple social networks. OS X enables you to take a single Photo Booth picture and use it to update your profile picture for Facebook, Twitter, and LinkedIn.

Update Your Social Network Profile Picture

1 Use Photo Booth to take a picture.

2 Click the picture you want to use.

3 Click **Share** (⬆).

4 Click **Change Profile Picture**.

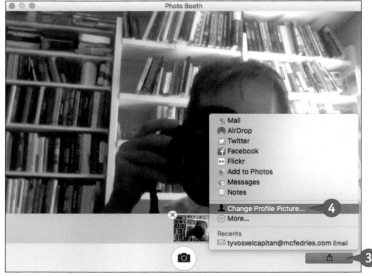

5 Drag the photo to the position you want.

6 Use this slider to set the magnification you want.

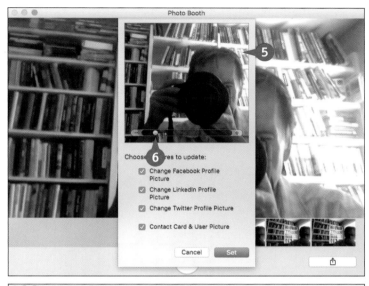

Photo Booth asks which profile you want to update.

7 Click to deselect the profile pictures you do not want to update (☑ changes to ☐).

8 Click **Set**.

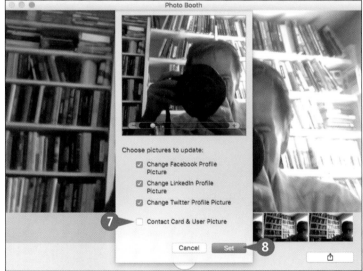

Can I update my Facebook profile picture from Photos?

Not directly, but you can use Photos to share an image to a Facebook album, and then use Facebook to set that image as your profile picture. In Photos, click the photo you want to use for your Facebook profile picture, click **Share** (⬆), and then click **Facebook**. In the Facebook share sheet, select **Only Me** in the left pop-up and choose an album in the right pop-up. Click **Post**. Log in to Facebook, click the photo you shared, hover the mouse (⬉) over the photo, and then click **Make Profile Picture**. Facebook updates your profile picture.

Connect to Your Flickr Account

Tens of millions of people use Flickr to share their photos with the world. If you have a Flickr account, you can use it to share photos directly from OS X, which comes with built-in support for Flickr. This enables you to send photos from many OS X apps, including Finder, Preview, Photos, and Photo Booth. Before you can send photos, you must sign in to your Flickr account.

Connect to Your Flickr Account

1 Click **System Preferences** (⊚).

Note: You can also click **Apple** (🍎) and then click **System Preferences**.

The System Preferences appear.

2 Click **Internet Accounts**.

The Internet Accounts preferences appear.

3 Click **Flickr**.

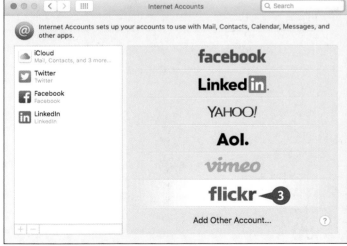

System Preferences prompts you for your Yahoo! ID and password.

4 Type your Yahoo! ID.

Note: Your Yahoo! ID is the email address associated with your Yahoo! account.

5 Type your Flickr password.

6 Click **Sign In**.

OS X signs in to your Flickr account.

Can I temporarily disable my Flickr account?

Yes. This is a useful technique if you know you will not be using your Flickr account for a while because it reduces clutter in the OS X sharing menus. To disable Flickr, follow steps **1** and **2** to open the Internet Accounts window. Click your Flickr account and then click the **Enable This Account** check box (☑ changes to ☐). Note that you can also use this technique to disable your Facebook, LinkedIn, and Vimeo accounts, if needed.

Send Photos to Flickr

Flickr is all about sharing your photos, so once you have connected OS X to your Flickr account, you can begin using that connection to upload photos. You can upload individual photos to Flickr using Finder, Quick Look, Preview, or Photo Booth, and those photos appear as part of your Flickr Photostream or an album. Similarly, you can upload multiple photos or an album from the Photos app, and you can add those photos to an existing Flickr album.

Send Photos to Flickr

1 In Finder, Quick Look, Preview, or Photo Booth, select or open the photo or photos you want to upload. In Photos, you can also select an album to upload.

2 Click **Share** (⬆).

3 Click **Flickr**.

OS X displays the Flickr share sheet.

A The photo appears inside the post.

4 Type a title.

5 Type a description.

6 Type one or more tags, separated by commas.

7 Click the **Access** and then click who can see the photo.

8 To add the photo to an album (also called a photo set), click the **Select Photo Set** and then click an album.

9 Click **Publish**.

OS X sends the photo to Flickr.

TIPS

Do I have to specify a Flickr album for my photo?

No. If you do not want the photo to appear in an album, or if you do not have a suitable album for the photo, do no choose anything from the Select Photo Set list. This tells Flickr to post the photo to your Photostream.

How can I upload my photos to a new Flickr album?

Unfortunately, you cannot do this within OS X. Instead, you need to sign in to your Flickr account on the web using Safari or another browser. Once you are signed in, open your albums and then click **Create new album**.

Set Up Your Vimeo Account

If you have a Vimeo account, you can use it to post videos online directly from OS X, which comes with built-in support for Vimeo. This enables you to send videos from many OS X apps, including Finder, QuickTime Player, Photo Booth, and iMovie. Before you can send videos, you must sign in to your Vimeo account.

Set Up Your Vimeo Account

1 Click **System Preferences** (⚙).

Note: You can also click **Apple** () and then click **System Preferences**.

The System Preferences appear.

2 Click **Internet Accounts**.

The Internet Accounts preferences appear.

3 Click **Vimeo**.

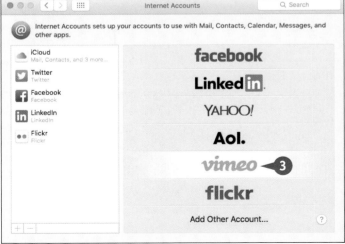

System Preferences prompts you for your Vimeo login data.

④ Type the email address associated with your Vimeo account.

⑤ Type your Vimeo password.

⑥ Click **Sign In**.

OS X signs in to your Vimeo account.

How do I delete my Vimeo account?

If you no longer use your Vimeo account, you should delete it from OS X. This not only reduces clutter in the OS X sharing menus, but also makes the Internet Accounts window easier to navigate.

To delete your Vimeo account, follow steps **1** and **2** to open the Internet Accounts window. Click your Vimeo account and then click **Remove** (—). When OS X asks you to confirm, click **OK**. Note that you can also use this technique to delete any other account that you no longer use.

Send a Video to Vimeo

Vimeo is one of the web's most popular video-sharing services, so once you have connected OS X to your Vimeo account, you can begin using that connection to upload videos. You have two ways to publish photos from OS X to Vimeo. First, you can use an OS X share sheet to upload a video to Vimeo using Finder, QuickTime Player, or Photo Booth. Second, you can upload a video to Vimeo from an iMovie project, which gives you many more options for publishing the video.

Send a Video to Vimeo

Send a Video Using a Share Sheet

1 In Finder, QuickTime Player, or Photo Booth, select or open the video you want to upload.

2 Click **Share** (🖰).

3 Click **Vimeo**.

OS X displays the Vimeo share sheet.

Ⓐ The attachment appears as a link inside the post.

4 Type a title.

5 Type a description.

6 Type one or more tags, separating each with a comma.

7 If you want anyone to be able to view the video, click the **Make this movie personal** check box (☑ changes to ☐).

8 Click **Publish**.

OS X sends the video to your Vimeo account.

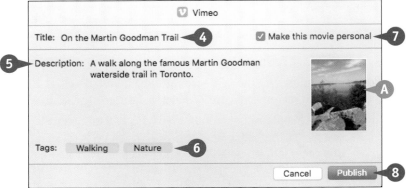

186

Send a Video from an iMovie Project

1 In iMovie, open the project you want to publish to Vimeo.

2 Click **Share**.

3 Click **Vimeo**.

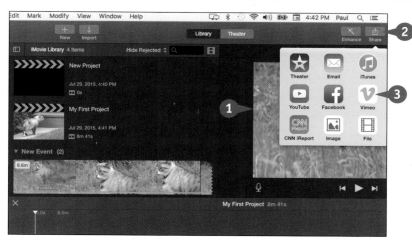

iMovie displays the Vimeo dialog.

4 Click **Sign In**, type your Vimeo email address and password, and then click **OK**.

5 Type a title.

6 Type a description.

7 Type one or more tags, separating each with a comma.

8 Select the movie size you want to use.

9 Click the **Viewable by** ☉ and then click with whom you want to share the video.

10 Click **Next**.

11 Click **Publish** (not shown).

iMovie uploads the video.

TIP

Do I have to sign in to Vimeo every time I want to upload a video using iMovie?

No, you can tell iMovie to save your sign-in data so that you do not have to enter it each time. In iMovie, click **Share** (⬆) and then click **Vimeo** to open the Vimeo dialog. Click **Sign In**, type your Vimeo email address and password, and then click to activate the **Remember this password in my keychain** check box (☐ changes to ☑). Click **OK**. The next time you click **Share** and then **Vimeo**, iMovie enters your Vimeo email address and password automatically.

Share Information with Other People

You can use OS X to share information with other people, including web pages, notes, pictures, videos, photos, and maps. OS X was built with sharing in mind. It comes with a feature called the *share sheet*, which not only enables you to easily share data via Facebook and Twitter, as you have seen in this chapter, but also via multiple other methods such as email and instant messaging.

Share Information with Other People

Share a Web Page

① Use Safari to navigate to the web page you want to share.

② Click **Share** (⬆).

③ Click the method you want to use to share the web page.

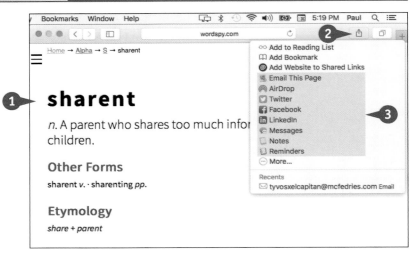

Share a Note

① In the Notes app, click the note you want to share.

② Click **Share** (⬆).

③ Click the method you want to use to share the note.

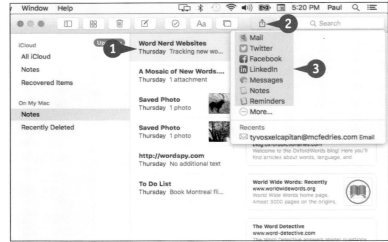

Share a Photos Picture

1. In Photos, click the picture you want to share.

2. Click **Share** (⬆).

3. Click the method you want to use to share the picture.

Share a Video

1. In QuickTime Player, open the video you want to share.

2. Click **Share** (⬆).

3. Click the method you want to use to share the video.

TIPS

Can I share a map or directions with my iPhone or iPad?
Yes. Maps and directions are usually much easier to use on a handheld device such as an iPhone or iPad. First, use the Maps app to display the map or the directions to a location. Click **Share** (⬆) and then click **Send to *Device***, where *Device* is the name of the device you want to use.

How do I share a Photo Booth photo?
Use Photo Booth to snap the photo using your Mac's attached camera. Click the photo, click **Share** (⬆), and then click the method you want to use to share the photo.

CHAPTER 10

Viewing and Editing Photos and Videos

Whether you want to look at your photos, or you want to edit them to fix problems, OS X comes with a number of useful tools for viewing and editing photos. It also offers tools for viewing digital videos.

View a Preview of a Photo

OS X offers several tools you can use to see a preview of any photo on your Mac. The Finder application has a number of methods you can use to view your photos, but here you learn about the two easiest methods. First, you can preview any saved image file using the OS X Quick Look feature; second, you can see photo previews by switching to the Cover Flow view. You can also preview photos using the Preview application.

View a Preview of a Photo

View a Preview with Quick Look

1 In Finder, open the folder that contains the photo you want to preview.

2 Click the photo.

3 Click **Quick Look** (👁) or press **Spacebar**.

Ⓐ Finder displays a preview of the photo.

View a Preview with Cover Flow

1 In Finder, open the folder that contains the photo you want to preview.

2 Click the photo.

3 Click **Cover Flow** (▯□▯).

Ⓑ Finder displays a preview of the photo.

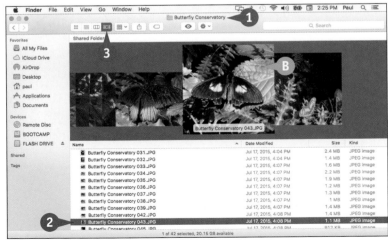

View a Preview in the Preview Application

1 In Finder, open the folder that contains the photo you want to preview.

2 Click the photo.

3 Click **File**.

4 Click **Open With**.

5 Click **Preview**.

Note: In many cases, you can also simply double-click the photo to open it in the Preview application.

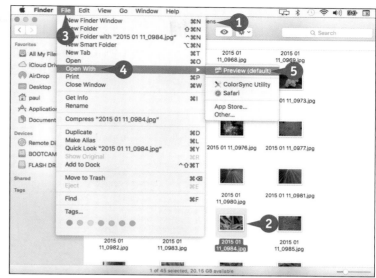

The Preview application opens and displays the photo.

6 Use the toolbar buttons to change how the photo appears in the Preview window.

C More commands are available on the View menu.

7 When you finish viewing the photo, click **Close** (●).

Is there an easier way to preview multiple photos using the Preview application?

Yes. In Finder, navigate to the folder that contains the photos and then select each file that you want to preview. Either click and drag the mouse (🖑) over the photos, or press and hold ⌘ and click each one. In Preview, press `Option`+`↓` and `Option`+`↑` to navigate the photos.

Is there a way that I can zoom in on just a portion of a photo?

Yes. In Preview, click and drag your mouse (🖑) to select the portion of the photo that you want to magnify. Click **View** and then click **Zoom to Selection** (or press ⌘+`*`).

View a Slideshow of Your Photos

Instead of viewing your photos one at a time, you can easily view multiple photos by running them in a slideshow. You can run the slideshow using the Preview application or Quick Look. The slideshow displays each photo for a few seconds and then Preview automatically displays the next photo. Quick Look also offers several on-screen controls that you can use to control the slideshow playback. You can also configure Quick Look to display the images full screen.

View a Slideshow of Your Photos

1 In Finder, open the folder that contains the photos you want to view in the slideshow.

2 Select the photos you want to view.

3 Click **File**.

4 Click **Open With**.

5 Click **Preview**.

The Preview window appears.

6 Click **View**.

7 Click **Slideshow**.

You can also select Slideshow by pressing Shift + ⌘ + F.

194

Preview opens the slideshow window.

⑧ Move the mouse (✛).

🅐 Preview displays the slideshow controls.

⑨ Click **Play** (▶).

Preview begins the slideshow.

🅑 You can click **Next** (⏭) to move to the next photo.

🅒 You can click **Back** (⏮) to move to the previous photo.

🅓 You can click **Pause** (⏸) to suspend the slideshow.

⑩ When the slideshow is over or when you want to return to Finder, click **Close** (✖) or press Esc.

Can I jump to a specific photo during the slideshow?
Yes. With the slideshow running, press Spacebar to stop the show. Use the arrow keys to select the photo that you want to view in the slideshow. Click **Play** to resume the slideshow.

What keyboard shortcuts can I use when viewing a slideshow?
Press ➡ or ⬆ to display the next photo, and press ⬅ or ⬇ to display the previous photo. Press Esc to end the slideshow.

Import Photos from a Digital Camera

You can import photos from a digital camera and save them on your Mac. You can use the Photos application to handle importing photos. Photos enables you to add a name and a description to each import, which helps you to find your photos after the import is complete. To perform the import, you need a cable to connect your digital camera to your Mac. Most digital cameras come with a USB cable. Note that the steps in this section also apply to importing photos from an iPhone or iPad.

Import Photos from a Digital Camera

Import Photos from a Digital Camera

1 Connect one end of the cable to the digital camera.

2 Connect the other end of the cable to a free USB port on your Mac.

3 Turn the camera on and put it in either playback or computer mode.

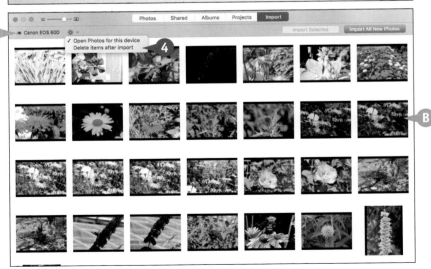

Your Mac launches the Photos application.

Note: You can also launch the application by clicking **Photos** (✷) in the Dock.

Ⓐ Your digital camera appears in the Devices section.

Ⓑ Photos displays previews of the camera's photos.

4 If you want Photos to remove the images from your camera after the import, click **Settings** (✷) and then click **Delete items after import**.

⑤ Click and drag the mouse (▶) around the photos you want, or press and hold ⌘ and click each photo you want to select.

⑥ Click **Import X Selected**, where *X* is the number of photos you selected in step **5**.

Ⓒ To import all the photos from the digital camera, click **Import All New Photos**.

Photos imports the photos from the digital camera.

View the Imported Photos

① Click **Albums**.

② Click **Last Import**.

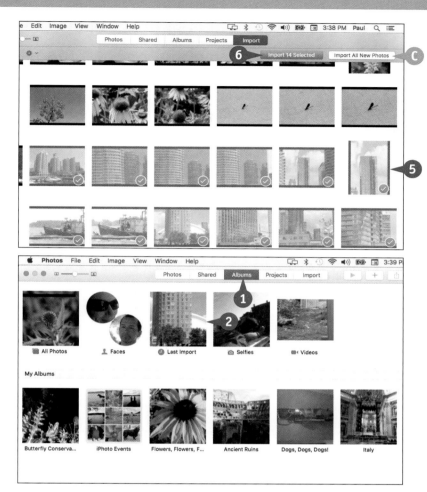

When I connect my digital camera, why do I see Image Capture instead of Photos?
Your Image Capture is not configured to open Photos when you connect your camera. To fix this, connect your digital camera to your Mac; the Image Capture application opens. (If you do not see the Image Capture application, click **Finder** (🙂) in the Dock, click **Applications**, and then double-click **Image Capture**.) Click the **Connecting** 🔽 and then click **Photos**. Click **Image Capture** in the menu bar and then click **Quit Image Capture**.

View Your Photos

If you want to look at several photos, you can use the Photos application. Photos offers a single-image view, which hides everything else and displays each photo using the entire height of the window. Once you activate the single-image view, Photos offers on-screen controls that you can use to navigate backward and forward through the photos. You can also configure single-image view to show thumbnail images of each photo, so you can quickly jump to any photo you want to view.

View Your Photos

① In the Photos application, click the **Photos** tab or press ⌘+1.

Ⓐ The Photos tab organizes your photos by *moments* — that is, by the date they were taken.

② Locate the date that contains the photos you want to view.

③ Double-click the first photo you want to view.

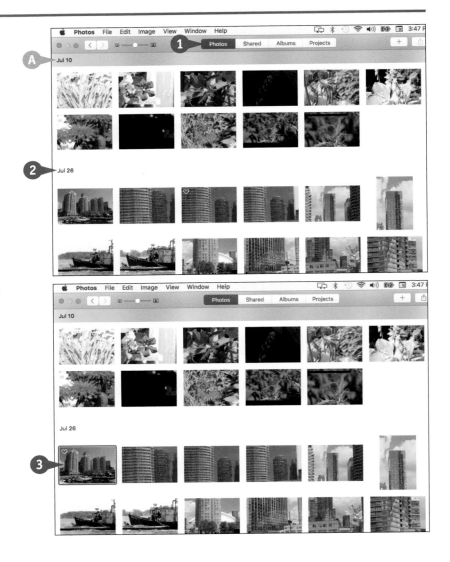

198

Photos displays the photo.

④ Click **Next** (>) to view the next photo.

Ⓑ You can also click **Previous** (<) to see the previous photo.

Note: You can also navigate photos by pressing ➡ and ⬅.

⑤ When you are done, click **Photos** or press ⌘+1 to return to the Photos tab.

TIP

Is there a way that I can jump quickly to a particular photo in full-screen mode?
Yes. Click **View** and then click **Show Split View** (or press Option+S). Photos uses the left side of the window to show thumbnails of the photos in the current date. Use the vertical scroll bar to bring the thumbnail of the photo you want into view. Click the photo's thumbnail. Photos displays the photo in full-screen mode.

Create an Album

You can use Photos to organize your photos into albums. In Photos, an *album* is a collection of photos that are usually related in some way. For example, you might create an album for a series of vacation photos, for photos taken at a party or other special event, or for photos that include a particular person, pet, or place. Using your Photos library, you can create customized albums that include only the photos that you want to view.

Create an Album

1 Click **New** (+).

Ⓐ To add an entire moment to a new album, move the mouse (▸) over the moment and then click **New** (+) beside the moment.

2 Click **Album**.

Note: You can also start a new album by pressing ⌘+N.

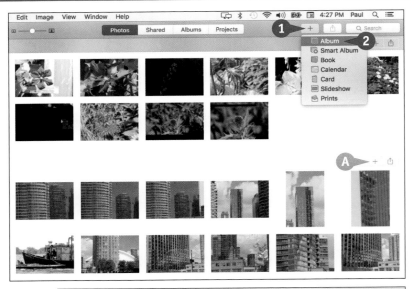

3 Type a name for the new album.

4 Click **OK**.

Photos prompts you to add items to the new album.

5 Click each photo you want to add to the album.

6 Click **Add**.

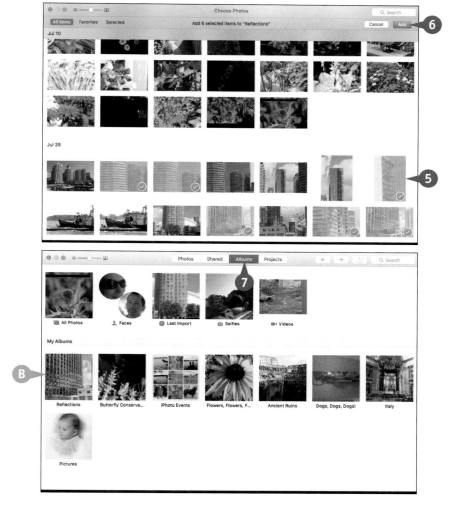

7 Click **Albums**.

B The new album appears in the My Albums section.

Is there any way to make Photos add photos to an album automatically?

Yes, you can create a *Smart Album* where the photos that appear in the album have one or more properties in common, such as the description, rating, date, or text in the photo title. Click **File** and then click **New Smart Album** (you can also press Option+⌘+N). Use the Smart Album dialog to create one or more rules that define what photos you want to appear in the album.

Crop a Photo

If you have a photo containing elements that you do not want to see, you can often cut out those elements. This is called *cropping*, and you can do this with the Photos app. When you crop a photo, you specify a rectangular area of the photo that you want to keep. Photos discards everything outside of the rectangle. Cropping is a useful skill because it can help give focus to the true subject of a photo. Cropping is also useful for removing extraneous elements that appear near the edges of a photo.

Crop a Photo

1 Open the photo you want to crop.

2 Click **Edit**.

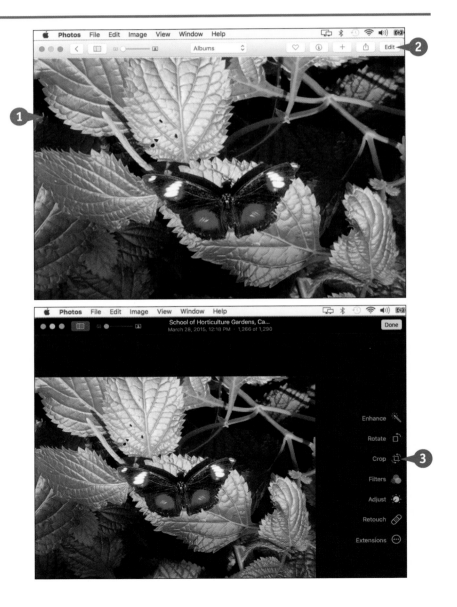

Photos displays its editing tools.

3 Click **Crop**.

Photos displays a cropping rectangle on the photo.

④ Click and drag a corner or side to define the area you want to keep.

Note: Remember that Photos keeps the area inside the rectangle.

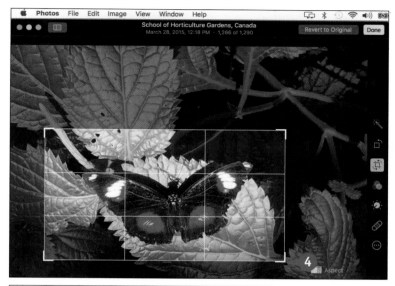

⑤ Click **Done**.

Photos saves the cropped photo and exits edit mode.

TIP

Is there a quick way to crop a photo to a certain size?
Yes, Photos enables you to specify either a specific shape, such as square, or a specific ratio, such as 4 x 3 or 16 x 9. Follow steps **1** to **3** to display the Crop tool. Click **Aspect** (Ⓐ) and then click the size or ratio you want to use. You can also click **Custom** (Ⓑ) to specify a custom ratio.

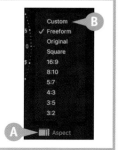

Rotate a Photo

You can rotate a photo using the Photos app. Depending on how you held your camera when you took a shot, the resulting photo might show the subject sideways or upside down. This may be the effect you want, but more likely this is a problem. To fix this problem, you can use Photos to rotate the photo so that the subject appears right-side up. You can rotate a photo either clockwise or counterclockwise.

Rotate a Photo

1 Open the photo you want to rotate.

Note: A quick way to rotate a photo is to right-click the photo and then click **Rotate Clockwise**.

2 Click **Edit**.

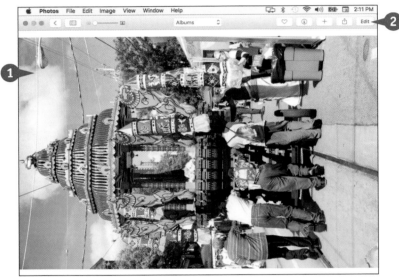

Photos displays its editing tools.

3 Click **Rotate**.

Ⓐ Photos rotates the photo 90 degrees counterclockwise.

④ Repeat step **3** until the subject of the photo is right-side up.

⑤ Click **Done**.

Photos saves your changes and exits edit mode.

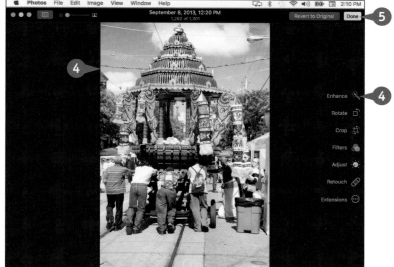

TIP

Can I rotate a photo clockwise instead?

Yes. With the editing tools displayed, press and hold Option. The Rotate icon changes from 🔄 to 🔄. Press and hold Option and then click **Rotate** to rotate the photo clockwise by 90 degrees. You can also right-click the photo and then click **Rotate Clockwise**.

Straighten a Photo

You can straighten a crooked photo using the Photos app. If you do not use a tripod when taking pictures, getting your camera perfectly level when you take a shot is very difficult and requires a lot of practice and a steady hand. Despite your best efforts, you might end up with a photo that is not quite level. To fix this problem, you can use Photos to nudge the photo clockwise or counterclockwise so that the subject appears straight.

Straighten a Photo

1 Open the photo you want to straighten.

2 Click **Edit**.

Photos displays its editing tools.

3 Click **Crop**.

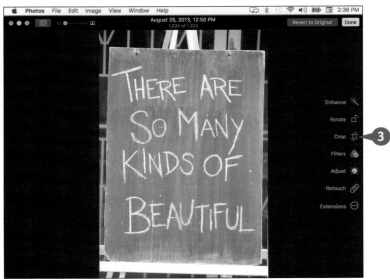

Photos displays its cropping and straightening tools.

④ Click and drag the **Angle** slider.

Drag the slider up to angle the photo counterclockwise.

Drag the slider down to angle the photo clockwise.

⑤ Click **Done**.

Photos saves your changes and exits edit mode.

How do I know when my photo is level?

Use the gridlines that Photos places over the photo while you drag the **Angle** slider. Locate a horizontal line in your photo and then rotate the photo so that this line is parallel to the nearest horizontal line in the grid. You can also match a vertical line in the photo with a vertical line in the grid.

Remove Red Eye from a Photo

You can remove red eye from a photo using the Photos app. When you use a flash to take a picture of one or more people, in some cases the flash may reflect off the subjects' retinas. The result is the common phenomenon of *red eye*, where each person's pupils appear red instead of black. If you have a photo where one or more people have red eyes due to the camera flash, you can use Photos to remove the red eye and give your subjects a more natural look.

Remove Red Eye from a Photo

1 Open the photo that contains the red eye.

2 Click **Edit**.

Photos displays its editing tools.

3 Click **Red-eye**.

Photos displays its Red-eye controls.

Ⓐ You may be able to fix the red eye automatically by clicking **Auto**. If that does not work, continue with the rest of these steps.

Ⓑ If needed, you can click and drag this slider to the right to zoom in on the picture.

④ Move the Red-Eye pointer over a red eye in the photo.

⑤ Click the red eye.

Ⓒ Photos removes the red eye.

⑥ Repeat steps **4** and **5** to fix any other instances of red eye in the photo.

⑦ Click **Done**.

Photos saves your changes and exits edit mode.

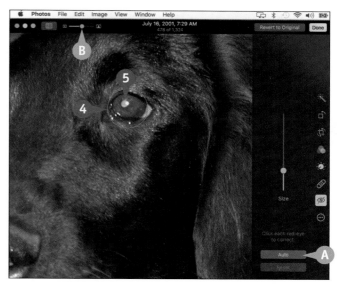

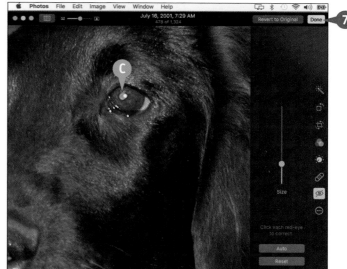

TIP

Why does Photos remove only part of the red eye in my photo?
The Red-Eye pointer may not be set to a large enough size. The tool should be approximately the same size as the subject's eye. If it is not, as shown here (Ⓐ), follow steps **1** to **3** to display the Red-eye controls. Click and drag the **Size** slider until the Red-Eye pointer is the size of the red-eye area. Use your mouse to move the circle over the red eye and then click.

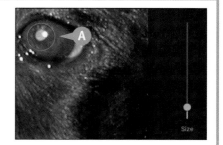

Add Names to Faces in Your Photos

You can make your photos easier to manage and navigate by adding names to the faces that appear in each photo. This is sometimes called *tagging*, and it enables you to navigate your photos by name.

Specifically, Photos includes a special Faces section in its library, which organizes your faces according to the names you assign when you tag your photos. This makes it easy to view all your photos in which a certain person appears.

Add Names to Faces in Your Photos

1 Open the photo that you want to tag.

2 Click **Show Info** (ⓘ).

Photos displays information about the photo.

3 Click **Add Faces**.

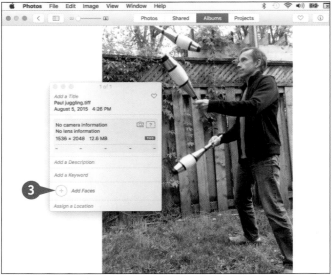

Photos displays its naming tools.

4 Click and drag the circle to center it on the person's face.

5 Click and drag this dot to size the circle to the person's face.

6 Click the **Click to Name** label.

7 Type the person's name.

8 Press **Return**.

9 Repeat steps **4** to **8** to name each person in the photo.

10 Click **Close** (●).

Photos saves the changes and exits naming mode.

TIP

How do I view all the photos that contain a particular person?
You can open a photo, click **Show Info** (ⓘ), and then double-click the person's face. You can also click the **Albums** tab and then double-click the **Faces** album. Photos displays the names and sample photos of each person you have named. Double-click the person you want to view. Photos displays all the photos that contain the person.

Mark Your Favorite Photos

You can make it easier and faster to find the photos you like best by marking those photos as favorites. If you take photos regularly, you can easily end up with hundreds or even thousands of images in your Photos library, and you might end up creating dozens of albums. Locating a cherished photo quickly becomes a time-consuming and frustrating chore. You can greatly speed up the task of locating such photos by marking them as favorites. Photos stores all your favorites in a special album, so it takes only a few clicks to view them.

Mark Your Favorite Photos

Mark a Single Photo

1 Open the photo that you want to mark as a favorite.

2 Click **Add to Favorites** (♡).

Photos marks the photo as a favorite.

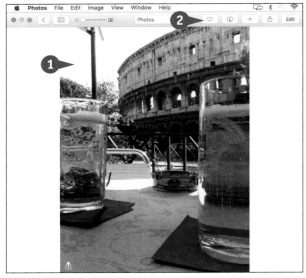

Mark Multiple Photos

1 Open the album that contains the photos you want to mark as favorites.

2 Press and hold ⌘ and click each photo you want to mark.

3 Click **Add to Favorites** (♡) in one of the selected photos.

Photos marks all the selected photos as favorites.

Note: To view your favorites, open the **Albums** tab and double-click the **Favorites** album.

Set an Album's Key Photo

You can make it easier to navigate your albums and to understand the content of your albums by setting the key photo for each album. The *key photo* is the image that appears in the Albums tab as the thumbnail used to display the album. As such, the key photo acts as a representative of all the photos in the album, so it should therefore either reflect the content of that album or contain text or an image that help you to identify the album.

Set an Album's Key Photo

1 Open the album you want to work with.

2 Double-click the image that you want to set as the album's key photo.

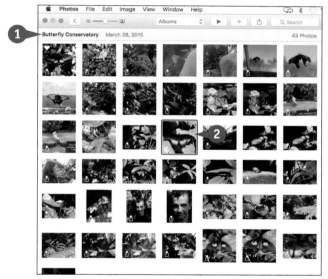

Photos opens the image.

3 Click **Image**.

4 Click **Make Key Photo**.

You can also press Shift+⌘+K.

Photos sets the image as the album's key photo.

Email a Photo

If you have a photo that you want to share with someone, and you know that person's email address, you can send the photo in an email message. Using Photos, you can specify what photo you want to send, and Photos creates a new message. Even if a photo is very large, you can still send it via email because you can use Photos to shrink the copy of the photo that appears in the message.

Email a Photo

1 Open the photo you want to send.

2 Click **Share** (□).

3 Click **Mail**.

A Photos creates a new message and adds the photo to the message body.

4 Type the address of the message recipient.

5 Type the message subject.

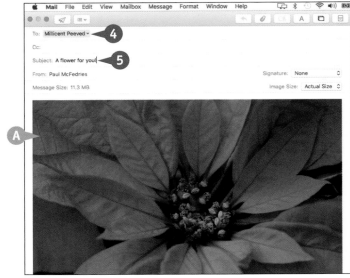

6 Click to the left of the image.

7 Press **Return** once or twice to move the image down.

8 Click here and then type your message text.

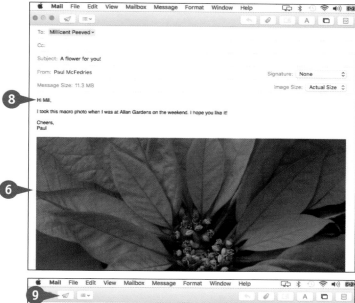

9 Click **Send** (✈).

Photos sends the message with the photo as an attachment.

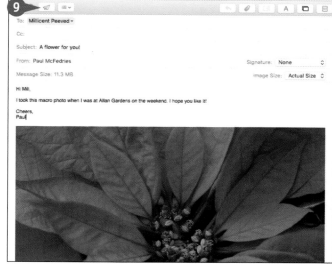

How do I change the size of the photo?

You need to be careful when sending photos because a single image can be several megabytes in size. If your recipient's email system places restrictions on the size of messages it can receive, your message might not go through.

To change the size of the photo, click the **Image Size** ⬧ and then click the size you want to use for the sent photo, such as Small or Medium. Note that this does not affect the size of the original photo, just the copy that is sent with the message.

Take Your Picture

You can use your Mac to take a picture of yourself. If your Mac comes with a built-in iSight or FaceTime HD camera, or if you have an external camera attached to your Mac, you can use the camera to take a picture of yourself using the Photo Booth application. After you take your picture, you can email that picture, add it to Photos, or set it as your user account or Messages buddy picture.

Take Your Picture

Take Your Picture with Photo Booth

1 Click **Spotlight** (Q).

2 Type **photo**.

3 Click **Photo Booth**.

The Photo Booth window appears.

Ⓐ The live feed from the camera appears here.

4 Click **Take a still picture** (☐).

Ⓑ Click **Take four quick pictures** (⊞) to snap four successive photos, each about 1 second apart.

Ⓒ Click **Take a movie clip** (▤) to capture the camera feed as a movie.

5 Click **Take Photo** (◉).

Photo Booth counts down 3 seconds and then takes the photo.

Work with Your Photo Booth Picture

D Photo Booth displays the picture.

1 Click the picture.

2 Click **Share** (⬆).

E You can click **Add to Photos** to add the image to the Photos app.

F You can click **Change profile picture** to set the photo as your user account picture.

Can I make my photos more interesting?

Definitely. Photo Booth comes with around two dozen special effects. Follow these steps:

1 Click **Effects**.

2 Click an icon to select a different page of effects.

A You can also use the arrows (◀ and ▶) to change pages.

3 Click the effect you want to use.

Play a DVD Using DVD Player

If your Mac has a DVD drive, you can insert a movie DVD into the drive and then use the DVD Player application to play the movie on your Mac. You can either watch the movie in full-screen mode, where the movie takes up the entire Mac screen, or play the DVD in a window while you work on other things. DVD Player has features that enable you to control the movie playback and volume.

Play a DVD Using DVD Player

Play a DVD Full Screen

1 Insert the DVD into your Mac's DVD drive.

DVD Player runs automatically and starts playing the DVD full screen.

Note: If DVD Player does not appear, click **Spotlight** (Q), type **dvd**, and then double-click **DVD Player**.

2 If you get to the DVD menu, click **Play** to start the movie.

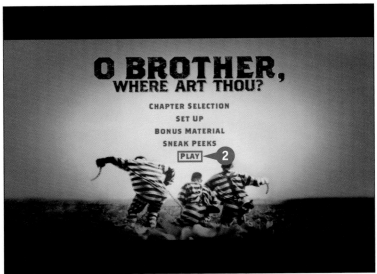

3 Move the mouse ( ) to the bottom of the screen.

The playback controls appear.

Ⓐ You can click ▌▌ to pause the movie.

Ⓑ You can click ▶▶ to fast-forward the movie.

Ⓒ You can click ◀◀ to rewind the movie.

Ⓓ You can drag the slider to adjust the volume.

Ⓔ You can click **menu** to display the DVD menu.

Ⓕ You can click to exit full-screen mode.

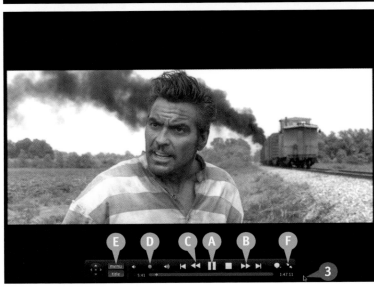

Play a DVD in a Window

1 Insert the DVD into your Mac's DVD drive.

DVD Player runs automatically and starts playing the DVD full screen.

2 Press ⌘+F.

Note: You can also press Esc or move the mouse (k) to the bottom of the screen and then click **Exit full screen**.

DVD Player displays the movie in a window.

G DVD Player displays the controller.

3 When you get to the DVD menu, click **Play** to start the movie.

H You can click ⏸ to pause the movie.

I You can click and hold ⏩ to fast-forward the movie.

J You can click and hold ⏪ to rewind the movie.

K You can drag the slider to adjust the volume.

L You can click **menu** to display the DVD menu.

M You can click ⏹ to stop the movie.

N You can click to eject the DVD.

TIP

How can I always start my DVDs in a window?
Press ⌘+F to switch to the window view. Click **DVD Player** in the menu bar, click **Preferences** to open the DVD Player preferences, and then click the **Player** tab. Click the **Enter Full Screen mode** check box (☑ changes to ☐). To manually control when the playback starts, click the **Start playing disc** check box (☑ changes to ☐). Click **OK** to put the new settings into effect.

Play Digital Video with QuickTime Player

OS X comes with an application called QuickTime Player that can play digital video files in various formats. You will mostly use QuickTime Player to play digital video files stored on your Mac, but you can also use the application to play digital video from the web.

QuickTime Player enables you to open video files, navigate the digital video playback, and control the digital video volume. Although you learn only how to play digital video files in this section, the version of QuickTime that comes with OS X comes with many extra features, including the capability to record movies and audio and to cut and paste scenes.

Play Digital Video with QuickTime Player

1 Click **Spotlight** (Q).

2 Type **quick**.

3 Click **QuickTime Player**.

The QuickTime Player application appears. If you see the Open dialog, skip to step **6**.

4 Click **File**.

5 Click **Open File**.

Note: You can also press ⌘+O.

The Open dialog appears.

6 Locate and click the video file you want to play.

7 Click **Open**.

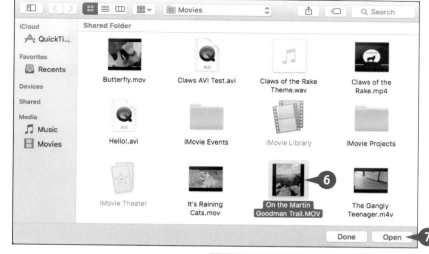

QuickTime opens a new player window.

8 Click **Play** (▶).

Ⓐ You can click ▶▶ to fast-forward the video.

Ⓑ You can click ◀◀ to rewind the video.

Ⓒ You can click and drag this slider to adjust the volume.

If you want to view the video in full-screen mode, press ⌘+F.

TIP

Can I use QuickTime Player to play a video from the web?
Yes. As long as you know the Internet address of the video, QuickTime Player can play most video formats available on the web. In QuickTime Player, click **File** and then click **Open Location** (or press ⌘+U). In the Open URL dialog, type or paste the video address in the Movie Location text box and then click **Open**.

CHAPTER 11

Securing OS X

Threats to your computing-related security and privacy often come from the Internet and from someone simply using your Mac while you are not around. To protect yourself and your family, you need to understand these threats and know what you can do to thwart them.

Change Your Password

You can make OS X more secure by changing your password. For example, if you turn on file sharing, as described in Chapter 15, you can configure each shared folder so that only someone who knows your password can get full access to that folder. Similarly, you should change your password if other network users know your current password and you no longer want them to have access to your shared folders. Finally, you should also change your password if you feel that your current password is too easy to guess. See the Tip to learn how to create a secure password.

Change Your Password

1 Click **System Preferences** (⬤).

The System Preferences appear.

2 Click **Users & Groups**.

The Users & Groups preferences appear.

Ⓐ Your user account is selected automatically.

Ⓑ If you want to work with a different user account, you must click the lock icon (🔒), type your administrator password (🔒 changes to 🔓), and then click the account.

3 Click **Change Password**.

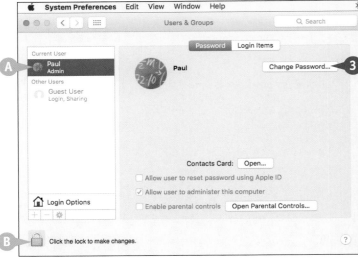

System Preferences asks whether you want to use your iCloud password.

4 Click **Change Password.**

C If you prefer to log in to OS X with your iCloud password, click **Use iCloud Password.**

The Change Password dialog appears.

5 Type your current password.

6 Type your new password.

7 Retype the new password.

8 Type a hint that OS X will display if you forget the password.

Note: Construct the hint in such a way that it makes the password easy for you to recall, but hard for a potential snoop to guess.

9 Click **Change Password.**

OS X changes your password.

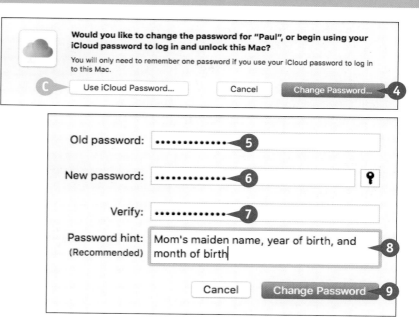

TIP

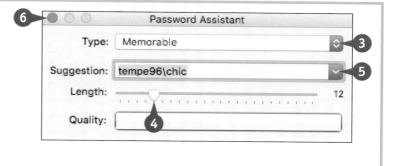

How do I create a secure password?
Follow these steps:

1 Follow steps 1 to 4 in this section.

2 Click **Password Assistant** (♀).

The Password Assistant dialog appears.

3 Click the **Type** ⊜ and then click a password type.

4 Click and drag the **Length** slider to set the password length you want to use.

5 Click the **Suggestion** ⌄ and then click the password you want to use.

6 Click **Close** (●).

Require a Password on Waking

You can enhance your Mac's security by configuring OS X to ask for your user account password when the system wakes up from either the screen saver or sleep mode. Protecting your account with a password prevents someone from logging on to your account, but what happens when you leave your Mac unattended? If you remain logged on to the system, any person who sits down at your computer can use it to view and change files.

To prevent this, activate the screen saver or sleep mode before you leave your Mac unattended, and configure OS X to require a password on waking.

Require a Password on Waking

1 Click **Apple** (⌘).

2 Click **System Preferences**.

You can also click **System Preferences** (◉) in the Dock.

The System Preferences appear.

3 Click **Security & Privacy**.

The Security & Privacy preferences appear.

④ Click the **General** tab.

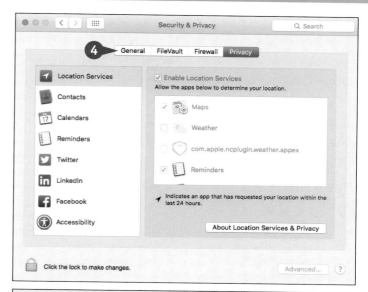

⑤ Click the **Require password** check box (☐ changes to ☑).

⑥ Click **Close** (●).

OS X puts the new setting into effect.

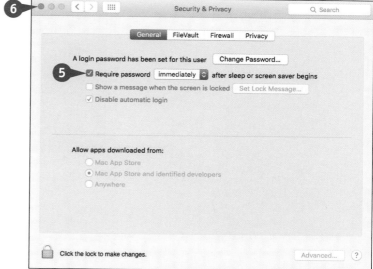

How do I activate the screen saver or sleep mode before I leave my Mac unattended?

To put your Mac display to sleep, press Control + Shift and then press the eject key (⏏). To engage full sleep mode, click **Apple** ( ) and then click **Sleep**.

If I engage the screen saver or sleep mode accidentally, entering my password is a hassle. Is there a workaround for this?

Yes, you can tell OS X to not require the password as soon as the screen saver or sleep mode is activated. Follow steps 1 to 5, click the **Require password** ⬦, and then click the amount of time you want OS X to wait.

Disable Automatic Logins

You can enhance your Mac's security by preventing OS X from logging in to your user account automatically. If you are the only person who uses your Mac, you can configure OS X to automatically log in to your account. This saves time at startup by avoiding the login screen, but it opens a security hole. If a snoop or other malicious user has access to your Mac, that person can start the computer and gain access to your documents, settings, web browsing history, and network. To prevent this, configure OS X to disable the automatic login.

Disable Automatic Logins

① Click **Apple** (🍎).

② Click **System Preferences**.

You can also click **System Preferences** (⚙) in the Dock.

The System Preferences appear.

③ Click **Security & Privacy**.

The Security & Privacy preferences appear.

④ Click the lock icon (🔒).

OS X prompts you for your administrator password.

⑤ Type the administrator password.

⑥ Click **Unlock**.

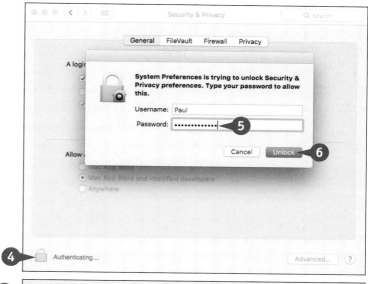

OS X unlocks the preferences (🔒 changes to 🔓).

⑦ Click the **General** tab.

⑧ Click the **Disable automatic login** check box (☐ changes to ☑).

⑨ Click **Close** (⚫).

OS X puts the new setting into effect.

TIP

Is there a way to get OS X to log out of my account automatically?
Yes, you can configure the system to log you out of your account when OS X has been idle for a specified amount of time. Follow steps **1** to **7** to unlock and display the General tab and then click **Advanced**. In the dialog that appears, click the **Log out after _X_ minutes of inactivity** check box (☐ changes to ☑) and then use the spin box to set the amount of idle time after which OS X logs you out automatically. You can select a time as short as 5 minutes and as long as 960 minutes.

Configure App Downloads

You can ensure that malware cannot be installed on your Mac by configuring the system to allow only app downloads from the Mac App Store. By default, OS X allows downloads from the App Store and from so-called *identified developers*. The reason for this heightened security is that malware developers are starting to target Macs now that they have become so popular. The extra security is a response to that and is designed to prevent users from accidentally installing malware. However, you can configure this feature to be even more secure, which is useful if you are setting up a user account for a child.

Configure App Downloads

1 Click **Apple** (🍎).

2 Click **System Preferences**.

You can also click **System Preferences** (🟤) in the Dock.

The System Preferences appear.

3 Click **Security & Privacy**.

The Security & Privacy preferences appear.

④ Click the lock icon (🔒).

OS X prompts you for your administrator password.

⑤ Type the administrator password.

⑥ Click **Unlock**.

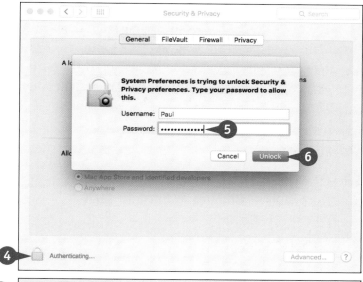

OS X unlocks the preferences (🔒 changes to 🔓).

⑦ Click the **General** tab.

⑧ Click the **Mac App Store** option (○ changes to ◉).

⑨ Click **Close** (●).

OS X puts the new setting into effect.

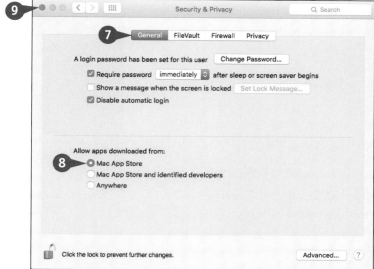

What is an identified developer?

An *identified developer* has registered with Apple and has a security certificate for digitally signing apps, thus certifying where the apps came from. It is possible a malicious developer could spoof a digitally signed app, so allowing only App Store apps is the safest option.

How can I install an app that I downloaded from the web?

If you are certain the app is legitimate — it was created by a reputable developer and purchased from a reputable dealer — double-click the downloaded file to open the disk image. Right-click (or Control-click) the installer, click **Open**, and then click **Open** when OS X asks you to confirm.

Turn On the Firewall

You can make your Mac's Internet connection much more secure by turning on the OS X firewall. A *firewall* is a tool designed to prevent malicious users from accessing a computer connected to the Internet. Chances are your network router already implements a hardware firewall, but you can add an extra layer of protection by also activating the OS X software firewall. This will not affect your normal Internet activities, such as web browsing, emailing, and instant messaging.

Turn On the Firewall

1 Click **Apple** (🍎).

2 Click **System Preferences**.

You can also click **System Preferences** (🖲) in the Dock.

The System Preferences appear.

3 Click **Security & Privacy**.

The Security & Privacy preferences appear.

④ Click the lock icon (🔒).

OS X prompts you for your administrator password.

⑤ Type the administrator password.

⑥ Click **Unlock**.

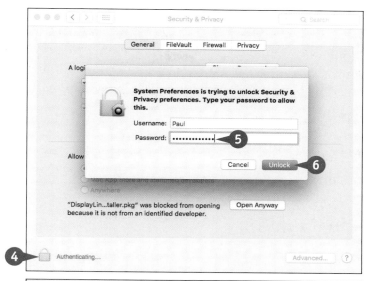

OS X unlocks the preferences (🔒 changes to 🔓).

⑦ Click the **Firewall** tab.

⑧ Click **Turn On Firewall**.

⑨ Click **Close** (🔴).

OS X puts the new setting into effect.

Can I prevent online malicious users from finding my Mac?

Yes. Malicious users often probe connected machines for vulnerabilities, so put OS X into *stealth mode*, which hides it from these probes. Follow steps **1** to **7**, click **Firewall Options**, click the **Enable stealth mode** check box (☐ changes to ☑), and then click **OK**.

Can I use Internet apps such as my FTP program through the firewall?

OS X allows digitally signed apps to receive connections, but to use an Internet app that is not digitally signed you must add it as an exception. Follow steps **1** to **7**, click **Firewall Options**, click **Add** (+), click the application you want to use, and then click **Add**.

Configure Location Services

Location services refers to the features and technologies that provide apps and system tools with access to location data, particularly the current location of your Mac. This is a handy and useful thing, but it is also something that you need to keep under your control because your location data, especially your current location, is fundamentally private and should not be given to applications thoughtlessly. Fortunately, OS X comes with a few tools for controlling and configuring location services.

Configure Location Services

1 Click **Apple** (🍎).

2 Click **System Preferences**.

You can also click **System Preferences** (⚙) in the Dock.

The System Preferences appear.

3 Click **Security & Privacy**.

The Security & Privacy preferences appear.

④ Click the lock icon (🔒).

OS X prompts you for your administrator password.

⑤ Type the administrator password.

⑥ Click **Unlock**.

OS X unlocks the preferences (🔒 changes to 🔓).

⑦ Click the **Privacy** tab.

⑧ Click **Location Services**.

⑨ Click the check box beside each app that you do not want to determine your location (✓ changes to ☐).

Note: This list will be empty if none of your apps have requested to use location services.

⑩ Click **Close** (●).

OS X puts the new setting into effect.

TIPS

How does the location services feature know my location?

Location services uses several bits of data to determine your location. First, it looks for known Wi-Fi networks that are near your location. Second, if you are connected to the Internet, it uses the location information embedded in your unique Internet Protocol (IP) address.

Can I turn off location services?

Yes. Follow steps **1** to **7** to unlock and display the Privacy tab. Click **Location Services** and then click the **Enable Location Services** check box (✓ changes to ☐). Note, however, that by turning off location services, you disable many features in apps such as Reminders and Maps.

Encrypt Your Data

By encrypting data, you can ensure that a malicious user who has physical access to your Mac cannot read the files in your user account. This means that your data appears as gibberish until it is decrypted by entering your user account password. Your password protects your user account from unauthorized access, but a sophisticated user can still access your data by using special tools. If you have sensitive, secret, or private files in your user account, you can protect that data from such access by encrypting it.

Encrypt Your Data

1 Follow steps **1** to **6** in the previous section, "Configure Location Services," to display and unlock the Security & Privacy preferences.

2 Click the **FileVault** tab.

3 Click **Turn On FileVault**.

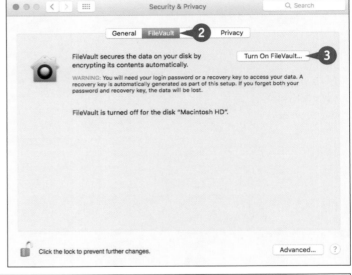

System Preferences asks whether you want to use your iCloud to unlock your disk if you forget your encryption password.

4 Click the **Allow my iCloud account to unlock my disk** option (○ changes to ⦿).

5 Click **Continue**.

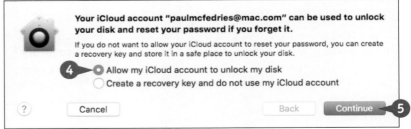

If you have multiple users, OS X prompts you to enable FileVault for the other accounts.

Ⓐ If you want to enable FileVault for a user, click **Enable User**, type the account password, and then click **OK**.

⑥ Click **Continue**.

OS X prompts you to restart the computer.

⑦ Click **Restart**.

OS X restarts and begins encrypting your user account data.

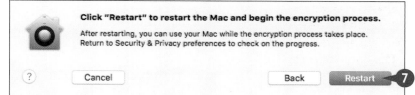

TIP

How do I encrypt my disk if I do not have an iCloud account?

In this case, OS X generates a *recovery key*, which is a code that you enter to unlock your disk if you forget your password. Follow steps **1** to **3** and click the **Create a recovery key and do not use my iCloud account** option (⃝ changes to ⦿), and then click **Continue**. When you see the recovery key, write it down and then continue with steps **5** to **7**. Store the recovery key in a secure, offsite location, such as a safety deposit box. If you lose the recovery key, you lose access to your data.

CHAPTER 12

Customizing OS X

OS X comes with a number of features that enable you to customize your Mac. For example, you might not like the default desktop background or the layout of the Dock. Not only can you change the appearance of OS X to suit your taste, but you can also change the way OS X works to make it easier and more efficient for you to use.

Display System Preferences

You can find many of the OS X customization features in System Preferences, a collection of settings and options that control the overall look and operation of OS X. You can use System Preferences to change the desktop background, specify a screen saver, set your Mac's sleep options, add user accounts, and customize the Dock, to name some of the tasks that you learn about in this chapter. To use these settings, you must know how to display the System Preferences window.

Display System Preferences

Open System Preferences

1 In the Dock, click **System Preferences** (⚙).

The System Preferences appear.

Close System Preferences

1 Click **System Preferences**.

2 Click **Quit System Preferences**.

TIPS

Are there other methods I can use to open System Preferences?
If you have hidden the Dock (see the section "Hide the Dock") or removed the System Preferences icon from the Dock, you can click **Apple** () and then click **System Preferences**.

Sometimes when I open System Preferences, I do not see all the icons. How can I restore the original icons?
When you click an icon in System Preferences, the window changes to show just the options and settings associated with that icon. To return to the main System Preferences window, click until the window appears. You can also click **Show All** () or press + .

Change the Desktop Background

To give OS X a different look, you can change the default desktop background. OS X offers a wide variety of desktop background options. For example, OS X comes with several dozen images you can use, from abstract patterns to photos of plants and other natural images. You can also choose a solid color as the desktop background, or you can use one of your own photos. You can change the desktop background to show either a fixed image or a series of images that change periodically.

Change the Desktop Background

Set a Fixed Background Image

1 In the Dock, click **System Preferences** (🔘) (not shown).

2 In the System Preferences, click **Desktop & Screen Saver**.

Note: You can also right-click (or `Control`-click) the desktop and then click **Change Desktop Background**.

The Desktop & Screen Saver preferences appear.

3 Click **Desktop**.

4 Click the image category you want to use.

Ⓐ To add a folder, click **Add** (➕), open the folder, and then click **Choose**.

5 Click the image you want to use as the desktop background.

Your Mac changes the desktop background.

6 If you chose a photo in step **5**, click ⬦ and then click an option to determine how your Mac displays the photo.

Note: Another way to set a fixed background image is to select a photo in the Photos app, click **Share** (⬆), and then click **Set Desktop**.

Set a Changing Background Image

1 Click the **Change picture** check box (☐ changes to ☑).

2 Click ⬦ and then click how often you want the background image to change.

3 If you want your Mac to choose the periodic image randomly, click the **Random order** check box (☐ changes to ☑).

Your Mac changes the desktop background periodically based on your chosen interval.

TIP

How do the various options differ for displaying a photo?
Your Mac gives you five options: **Fill Screen** expands the photo in all four directions until it fills the entire desktop. **Fit to Screen** expands the photo in all four directions until the photo is either the same height as the desktop or the same width as the desktop. **Stretch to Fill Screen** expands the photo in all four directions until it fills the entire desktop. **Center** displays the photo at its actual size and places the photo in the center of the desktop. **Tile** repeats your photo multiple times to fill the entire desktop.

Set Your Mac's Sleep Options

You can make OS X more energy-efficient by configuring parts of your Mac to go into sleep mode automatically when you are not using them. *Sleep mode* means that your display or your Mac is in a temporary low-power mode. This saves energy on all Macs, and saves battery power on a notebook Mac. For example, you can set up OS X to put the display to sleep automatically after a period of inactivity. Similarly, you can configure OS X to put your entire Mac to sleep after you have not used it for a specified amount of time.

Set Your Mac's Sleep Options

Open the Energy Saver Preferences

1 In the Dock, click **System Preferences** (⚙) (not shown).

2 In the System Preferences, click **Energy Saver**.

The Energy Saver preferences appear.

Set Sleep Options for a Desktop Mac

1 Click and drag the slider to set the display sleep timer.

This specifies the period of inactivity after which your display goes to sleep.

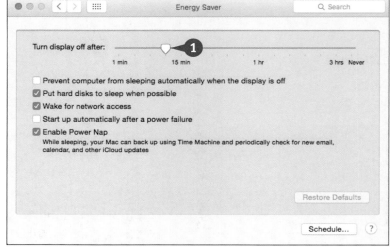

Set Sleep Options for a Notebook Mac

1 Click **Battery**.

2 Click and drag the slider to set the computer sleep timer for when your Mac is on battery power.

3 Click and drag the slider to set the display sleep timer for when your Mac is on battery power.

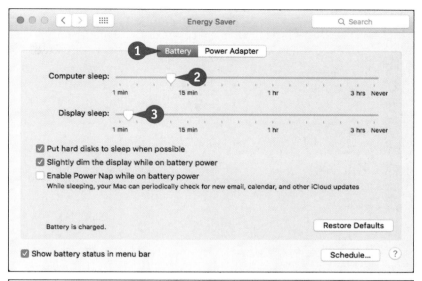

4 Click **Power Adapter**.

5 Click and drag the slider to set the computer sleep timer for when your Mac is plugged in.

6 Click and drag the slider to set the display sleep timer for when your Mac is plugged in.

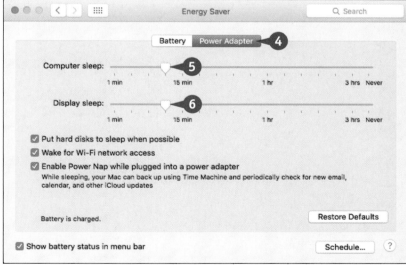

TIPS

How do I wake a sleeping display or computer?

If your Mac's display is in sleep mode, you can wake it by moving your mouse (🖐) or sliding your finger on the trackpad. You can also wake up the display or your entire Mac by pressing any key.

I changed the display sleep timer, and now I never see my screen saver. Why?

You set the display sleep timer to less than your screen saver timer. For example, if you configured the screen saver timer to 15 minutes and the display sleep timer to 10 minutes, OS X always puts the display to sleep before the screen saver appears.

Change the Display Resolution and Brightness

You can change the resolution and the brightness of the OS X display. This enables you to adjust the display for best viewing or for maximum compatibility with whatever application you are using.

Increasing the display resolution is an easy way to create more space on the screen for applications and windows, because the objects on the screen appear smaller. Conversely, if you have trouble reading text on the screen, decreasing the display resolution can help because the screen objects appear larger. If you find that your display is too dark or too bright, you can adjust the brightness for best viewing.

Change the Display Resolution and Brightness

1 In the Dock, click **System Preferences** (⚙) (not shown).

2 In the System Preferences, click **Displays**.

The Displays preferences appear.

3 Click **Display**.

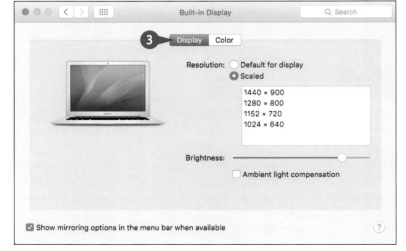

4 Select the resolution:

A To have OS X set the resolution based on your display, click the **Default for display** option (⭕ changes to ⦿).

B To set the resolution yourself, click the **Scaled** option (⭕ changes to ⦿) and then click the resolution you want to use.

OS X adjusts the screen to the new resolution.

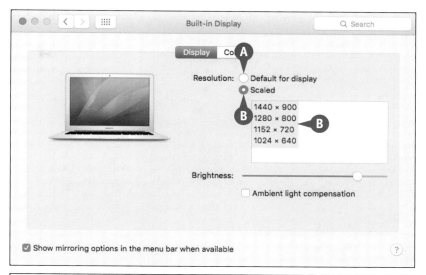

5 For some screens, you can click and drag the **Brightness** slider to set the display brightness.

OS X adjusts the screen to the new brightness.

C If you do not want OS X to adjust the notebook screen brightness based on the ambient light, click the **Ambient light compensation** check box (☑ changes to ☐).

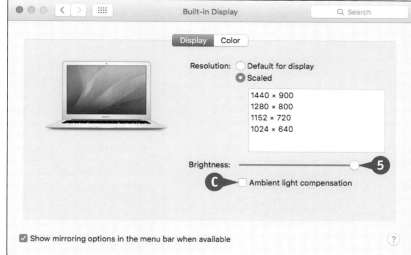

TIPS

What do the resolution numbers mean?
These numbers are expressed in *pixels*, which are the individual dots that make up what you see on your Mac's screen, arranged in rows and columns. So a resolution of 1440 x 900 means that the display is using 1,440-pixel rows and 900-pixel columns.

Why do some resolutions also include the word "stretched"?
Most older displays use an aspect ratio (width to the height) of 4:3. However, most new displays use a *widescreen* aspect ratio of either 16:9 or 16:10. Resolutions designed for 4:3 displays use only part of a widescreen display. To make them use the entire display, choose the *stretched* version of the resolution, although in some cases this may distort screen text and images.

Create an App Folder in Launchpad

You can make Launchpad easier to use by combining multiple icons into a single storage area called an *app folder*. Normally, Launchpad displays icons in up to five rows per screen, with at least seven icons in each row, so you can have at least 35 icons in each screen. Also, if you have configured your Mac with a relatively low display resolution, you might see only partial app names in Launchpad.

All this can make it difficult to locate your apps. However, app folders can help you organize similar apps and reduce the clutter on the Launchpad screens.

Create an App Folder in Launchpad

① Click **Launchpad** (🚀).

Ⓐ Launchpad displays icons for each installed application.

② Click the dot for the Launchpad screen you want to work with.

③ Click and drag an icon that you want to include in the folder, and drop it on another icon that you want to include in the same folder.

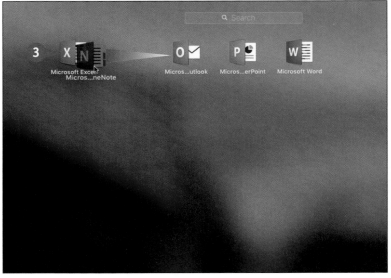

Launchpad creates the app folder.

B Launchpad applies a name to the folder based on the type of applications in the folder.

C Launchpad adds the icons to the app folder.

D To specify a different name, you can click the name and then type the one you prefer.

4 Click the Launchpad screen, outside of the app folder.

E Launchpad displays the app folder.

5 To add more icons to the new app folder, click and drag each icon and drop it on the folder.

Note: To launch a program from an app folder, click **Launchpad** (🚀), click the app folder to open it, and then click the program's icon.

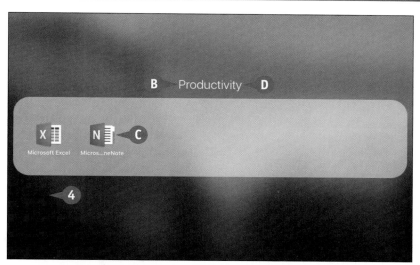

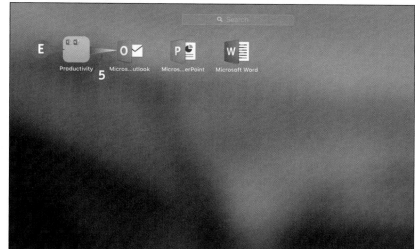

TIPS

How do I make changes to an app folder?
Open Launchpad and then click the app folder. To rename the folder, click the current name, type the new name, and then press `Return`. To rearrange the icons, drag and drop the apps within the folder. When you are done, click outside the app folder.

How do I remove an icon from an app folder?
Open Launchpad and then click the app folder. To remove an app, click and drag the app out of the folder. Launchpad closes the folder, and you can then drop the icon within the Launchpad screen.

Add a User Account

You can share your Mac with another person by creating a user account for that person. This enables the person to log in to OS X and use the system. The new user account is completely separate from your own account. This means that the other person can change settings, create documents, and perform other OS X tasks without interfering with your own settings or data. For maximum privacy for all users, you should set up each user account with a password.

Add a User Account

① In the Dock, click **System Preferences** (⚙) (not shown).

② In the System Preferences, click **Users & Groups**.

Ⓐ In most OS X systems, to modify accounts you must click the lock icon (🔒) and then type your administrator password (🔒 changes to 🔓).

③ Click **Add** (+).

The New Account dialog appears.

4 Click the **New Account** ⬦ and then click an account type.

5 Type the user's name.

6 Edit the short username that OS X creates.

7 If the user has an iCloud account, click **Use iCloud password**; otherwise, click the **Use separate password** option (◯ changes to ◉).

8 Type and retype the user's password.

9 Type a hint that OS X will display if the user forgets the password.

10 Click **Create User**.

B OS X adds the user account to the Users & Groups preferences.

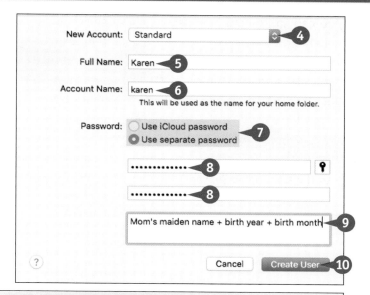

Which account type should I use for the new account?

The Standard type is a good choice because it can make changes only to its own account settings. Avoid the Administrator type because it enables the user to make major changes to the system. Consider the Managed with Parental Controls account type for children.

How do I change the user's picture?

Click the user and then click the picture. OS X displays a list of the available images. If you see one you like, click it. If your Mac has a camera attached and the user is nearby, you can click **Camera** and then click **Camera** (📷) to take the user's picture.

Customize the Dock

You can customize various aspects of the Dock by using System Preferences to modify a few Dock options. For example, you can make the Dock take up less room on the screen by adjusting the size of the Dock. You can also make the Dock a bit easier to use by turning on the Magnification feature, which enlarges Dock icons when you position the mouse (▸) over them. You can also make the Dock easier to access and use by moving it to either side of the screen.

Customize the Dock

1 In the Dock, click **System Preferences** (⚙).

2 In the System Preferences, click **Dock**.

Note: You can also open the Dock preferences by clicking **Apple** (), clicking **Dock**, and then clicking **Dock Preferences**.

The Dock preferences appear.

3 Click and drag the **Size** slider to make the Dock smaller or larger.

A You can also click and drag the Dock divider: Drag up to increase the Dock size, and drag down to decrease the Dock size.

B System Preferences adjusts the size of the Dock.

Note: If your Dock is already as wide as the screen, dragging the Size slider to the right (toward the Large value) has no effect.

252

④ Click the **Magnification** check box (☐ changes to ☑).

⑤ Click and drag the **Magnification** slider to set the magnification level.

⚪ When you position the mouse (🖱) over a Dock icon, your Mac magnifies the icon.

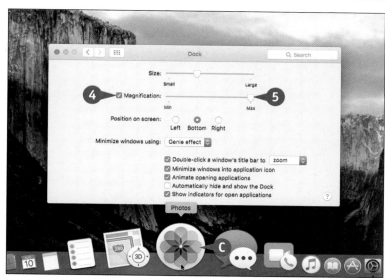

⑥ Use the **Position on screen** options to click where you want the Dock to appear, such as the **Left** side of the screen (◯ changes to ◉).

Ⓓ Your Mac moves the Dock to the new position.

⑦ Click the **Minimize windows using** ⬦ and then click the effect you want your Mac to use when you minimize a window by clicking ⚪: **Genie effect** or **Scale effect**.

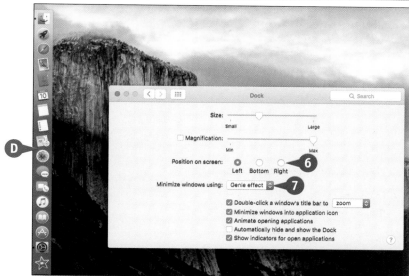

TIP

Is there an easier method I can use to control some of these preferences?
Yes, you can control these preferences directly from the Dock. To set the Dock size, click and drag the Dock divider left or right. For the other preferences, right-click (or **Control**-click) the Dock divider. Click **Turn Magnification On** to enable the magnification feature; click **Turn Magnification Off** to disable this feature. To change the Dock position, click **Position on Screen** and then click **Left**, **Bottom**, or **Right**. To set the minimize effect, click **Minimize Using** and then click either **Genie Effect** or **Scale Effect**.

Add an Icon to the Dock

The icons on the Dock are convenient because you can open them with just a single click. You can enhance the convenience of the Dock by adding an icon for an application you use frequently.

The icon remains in the Dock even when the application is closed, so you can always open the application with a single click. You can add an icon to the Dock even if the program is not currently running.

Add an Icon to the Dock

Add an Icon for a Nonrunning Application

1 Click **Finder** ( ).

2 Click **Applications**.

3 Click and drag the application icon, and then drop it inside the Dock.

Ⓐ Be sure to drop the icon anywhere to the left of the Dock divider.

B OS X adds the application's icon to the Dock.

Add an Icon for a Running Application

1 Right-click (or Control-click) the application icon in the Dock.

2 Click **Options**.

3 Click **Keep in Dock**.

The application's icon remains in the Dock even after you close the program.

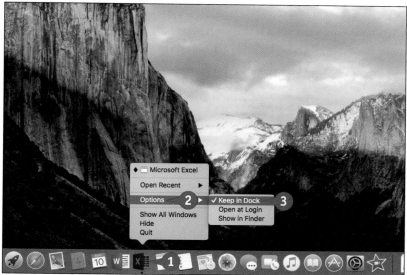

TIPS

Can my Mac start the application automatically each time I log in?

Yes. You can configure your application as a *login item*, which is a program or similar item that runs automatically after you log in. Right-click (or Control-click) the application's Dock icon, click **Options**, and then click **Open at Login**.

How do I remove an icon from the Dock?

Drag it off the Dock, or right-click (or Control-click) the application's Dock icon, click **Options**, and then click **Remove from Dock**. If the application is running, OS X removes the icon from the Dock when you quit the program. You can remove any application icon except Finder ( ).

Hide the Dock

When you are working in an application, you might find that you need to maximize the amount of vertical space the application window takes up on-screen. This might come up, for example, when you are reading or editing a long document or viewing a large photo. In such cases, you can size the window to maximum height, but OS X will not let you go past the Dock. You can work around this by hiding the Dock. When the Dock is hidden, it is still easily accessible whenever you need to use it.

Hide the Dock

Turn On Dock Hiding

1 Right-click (or **Control**-click) the Dock divider.

2 Click **Turn Hiding On**.

A OS X removes the Dock from the desktop.

Display the Dock Temporarily

1 Move the mouse (▶) to the bottom of the screen.

B OS X temporarily displays the Dock.

Note: To hide the Dock again, move the mouse (▶) away from the bottom of the screen.

TIPS

Is there a faster way to hide the Dock?
Yes. You can quickly hide the Dock by pressing `Option`+`⌘`+`D`. This keyboard shortcut is a toggle, which means that you can also turn off Dock hiding by pressing `Option`+`⌘`+`D`. When the Dock is hidden, you can display it temporarily by pressing `Control`+`F3` (on some keyboards you must press `Fn`+`Control`+`F3`).

How do I bring the Dock back into view?
When you no longer need the extra screen space for your applications, you can turn off Dock hiding to bring the Dock back into view. Display the Dock, right-click (or `Control`-click) the Dock divider, and then click **Turn Hiding Off**.

Add a Widget to the Notification Center

The Notification Center is an OS X application that you use not only to view your latest notifications, but also to display widgets. A widget is a mini-application, particularly one designed to perform a single task, such as displaying the weather, showing stock data, or working with reminders. You can customize the Notification Center to include any widgets that you find useful or informative. OS X comes with several widgets, and there are also many widgets available via the App Store.

Add a Widget to the Notification Center

1 Click **Notification Center** (☰).

2 Click **Today**.

OS X displays the Notification Center and its current set of widgets.

3 Click **Edit**.

OS X displays its collection of widgets.

4 Click **Add** (➕) beside the widget you want to add.

A OS X adds the widget to the Notification Center.

5 Click and drag the widget to the position you prefer.

6 Click **Done**.

OS X updates the Notification Center.

TIPS

Can I get more widgets?
Yes, the App Store has a section dedicated to Notification Center widgets, some of which are free. To see what is available, follow steps **1** to **3** to open the widgets list for editing and then click **App Store**.

How do I remove a widget from the Notification Center?
To remove a widget, follow steps **1** to **3** to open the widgets list for editing, and then click **Remove** (➖) that appears to the left of the widget. OS X removes the widget and adds it to the Items list, just in case you want to use it again later. Click **Done**.

Extend the Desktop Across Multiple Displays

You can improve your productivity and efficiency by connecting a second monitor to your Mac. To work with an extra display, your Mac must have a video output port — such as a Thunderbolt port or Mini DisplayPort — that matches a corresponding port on the second display. If you do not have such a port, check with Apple or the display manufacturer to see if an adapter is available that enables your Mac to connect with the second display. After you connect your Mac to the display, you can extend the OS X desktop across both monitors.

Extend the Desktop Across Multiple Displays

1 Connect the second monitor to your Mac.

2 Open System Preferences.

Note: See the section "Display System Preferences," earlier in this chapter.

3 Click **Displays**.

The Displays preferences appear.

4 Click **Arrangement**.

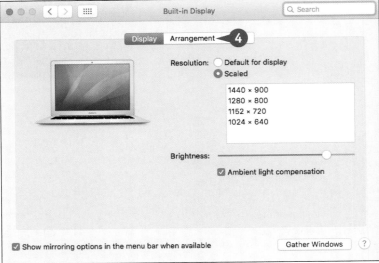

A This window represents your Mac's main display.

B This window represents the second display.

C This white strip represents the OS X menu bar.

5 Click and drag the windows to set the relative arrangement of the two displays.

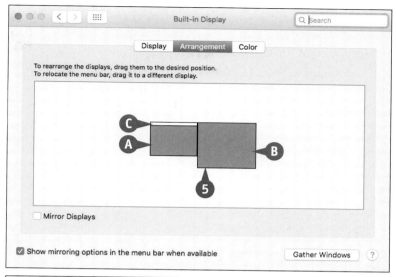

6 To move the menu bar and Dock to the second display, click and drag the menu bar and drop it on the second display.

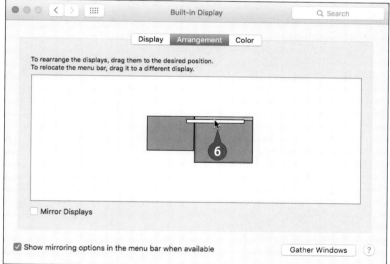

Can I use a different desktop background in each display?

Yes. To set the desktop background on the second display, open System Preferences and click **Desktop & Screen Saver**. On the second display, use the Secondary Desktop dialog to set the desktop picture or color, as described in the section "Change the Desktop Background."

Can I just use the second display to show my main OS X desktop?

Yes. This is called *mirroring* the main display because the second display shows exactly what appears on your Mac's main monitor, including the mouse pointer. Follow steps 1 to 4 to display the Arrangement tab and then click the **Mirror Displays** check box (changes to ✓).

Customize the Share Menu

The Share menu appears in many OS X applications, including Finder, Safari, Preview, Maps, and Notes. You use the Share menu's extensions to perform actions on the application's content. For example, in Safari you can use the Sharing menu to create a bookmark, send the page URL via email, text message, or AirDrop, or share the page on Twitter, Facebook, or LinkedIn. If you find that extensions are on the Share menu that you never use, you can reduce clutter on the menu by removing those items. You can also reorder the menu to put the items you use most often near the top.

Customize the Share Menu

Display the Share Menu Extensions

1 In the Dock, click **System Preferences** (⚙).

2 In the System Preferences, click **Extensions**.

The Extensions preferences appear.

3 Click **Share Menu**.

Ⓐ OS X displays the extensions available for the Share menu.

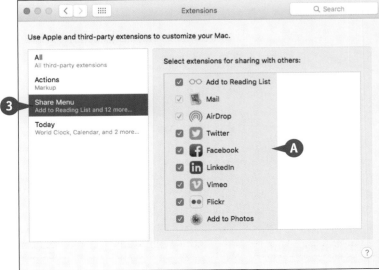

Remove a Share Menu Extension

1 To temporarily remove an extension from the Share menu, click its check box (☑ changes to ☐).

The next time you open the Share menu, you will no longer see the extension.

Note: OS X moves the disabled extension to the bottom of the list. To enable the extension later on, scroll to the bottom of the list and click the extension's check box (☐ changes to ☑).

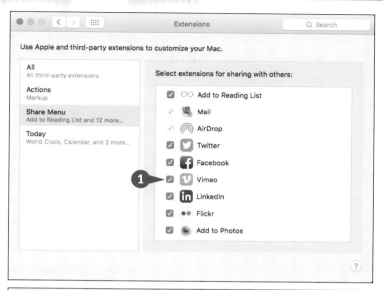

Move a Share Menu Extension

1 Position the mouse (▶) over the name of the icon of the extension you want to move (▶ changes to 🖐).

2 Click and drag the extension up or down to the new menu position and then release the extension.

The next time you open the Share menu, you will see the extension in its new position.

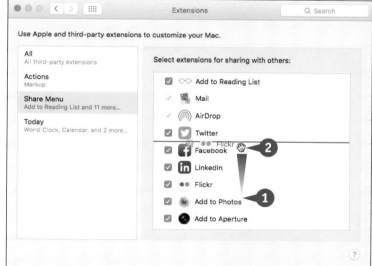

TIPS

Is there a quicker method I can use to customize the Share menu?
Yes, if you are working in an application that includes the Share menu. If so, click **Share** (🗂) and then click **More**. OS X automatically runs System Preferences, opens the Extensions preferences, and selects the Share Menu item.

What is the difference between the Share menu and a share sheet?
The Share menu is a list of OS X extensions that let share your data. When you select some Share menu items, such as Facebook or Twitter (see Chapter 9), OS X display a *share sheet*, which enables you to add extras such as text and location before you share the data.

CHAPTER 13

Maintaining OS X

To keep OS X running smoothly, maintain top performance, and reduce the risk of computer problems, you need to perform some routine maintenance chores. This chapter shows you how to empty the Trash, delete unnecessary files, uninstall applications, back up and restore your files, recondition your notebook battery, and more.

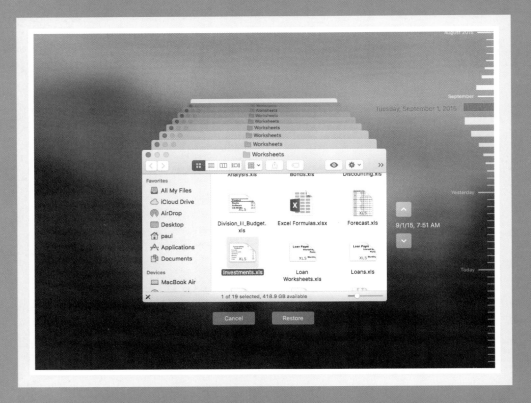

Empty the Trash

You can free up disk space on your Mac by periodically emptying the Trash. When you delete a file or folder, OS X does not immediately remove the file from your Mac's hard drive. Instead, OS X moves the file or folder to the Trash. This is useful if you accidentally delete an item because it means you can open the Trash and restore the item. However, all those deleted files and folders take up disk space, so you need to empty the Trash periodically to regain that space. You should empty the Trash at least once a week.

Empty the Trash

1 Click the desktop.

2 Click **Finder** from the menu.

3 Click **Empty Trash**.

Ⓐ You can also right-click **Trash** (🗑) and then click **Empty Trash**.

Note: Another way to select the Empty Trash command is to press `Shift`+`⌘`+`Delete`.

OS X asks you to confirm the deletion.

4 Click **Empty Trash**.

OS X empties the Trash (🗑 changes to 🗑).

Are you sure you want to permanently erase the items in the Trash?

You can't undo this action.

Cancel   Empty Trash 4

Organize Your Desktop

CHAPTER
13

You can make your OS X desktop easier to scan and navigate by organizing the icons. The OS X desktop automatically displays icons for objects such as your external hard drives, inserted CDs and DVDs, disk images, and attached iPods. The desktop is also a handy place to store files, file aliases, copies of documents, and more. However, the more you use your desktop as a storage area, the harder it is to find the icon you want. You can fix this by organizing the icons.

Organize Your Desktop

1 Click the desktop.

2 Click **View**.

3 Click **Clean Up By**.

4 Click **Name**.

You can also right-click the desktop, click **Clean Up By**, and then click **Name**, or press Option+⌘+1.

Ⓐ Your Mac organizes the icons alphabetically and arranges them in columns from right to left.

Check Hard Drive Free Space

To ensure that your Mac's hard drive does not become full, you should periodically check how much free space it has left. If you run out of room on your Mac's hard drive, you will not be able to install more applications or create more documents, and your Mac's performance will suffer. To ensure your free space does not become too low — say, less than about 50GB — you can check how much free space your hard drive has left.

You should check your Mac's hard drive free space about once a month.

Check Hard Drive Free Space

Check Free Space Using Finder

1. Click **Finder** (😀).

2. Click **Desktop**.

Note: You can also click any folder on your Mac's hard drive.

3. In the status bar, read the available value, which tells you the amount of free space left on the hard drive.

   If you do not see the status bar, press ⌘+/.

Display Free Space on the Desktop

1. Display your Mac's HD (hard drive) icon on the desktop, as described in the first Tip.

2. Click the desktop.

3. Click **View**.

4. Click **Show View Options**.

Note: You can also run the Show View Options command by pressing ⌘+J.

The Desktop dialog appears.

5 Click the **Show item info** check box (☐ changes to ☑).

A Your Mac displays the amount of free hard drive space under the Macintosh HD icon.

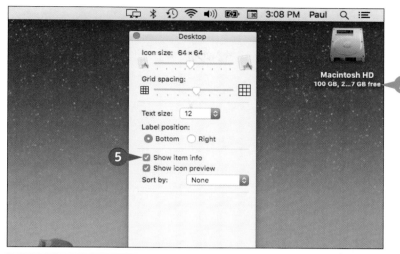

6 Drag the **Icon size** slider until you can read all the icon text.

7 If you still cannot read all the text, click the **Text size** ◌ and then click a larger size.

8 Click **Close** (●).

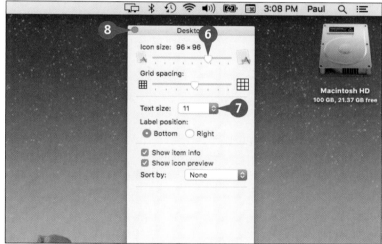

TIPS

My Mac's hard drive icon does not appear on the desktop. How do I display it?
Click the desktop, click **Finder** in the menu bar, and then click **Preferences**. Click the **General** tab, click the **Hard disks** check box (☐ changes to ☑), and then click **Close** (●).

What should I do if my Mac's hard drive space is getting low?
First, empty the Trash, as described earlier in this chapter. Next, uninstall applications you no longer use, as described in the next section. If you have large documents you no longer need, either move them to an external hard drive or flash drive, or delete them and then empty the Trash.

Uninstall Unused Applications

If you have an application that you no longer use, you can free up some disk space and reduce clutter in the Applications folder by uninstalling that application. When you install an application, the program stores its files on your Mac's hard drive, and although most programs are quite small, many require hundreds of megabytes of space. Uninstalling applications you do not need frees up the disk space they use and removes their icons or folders from the Applications folder. In most cases, you must be logged on to OS X with an administrator account to uninstall applications.

Uninstall Unused Applications

1 Click **Finder** ( ).

2 Click **Applications**.

3 Click and drag the application or its folder and drop it on **Trash** ( ).

OS X prompts you for an administrator password.

4 Type the password.

5 Click **OK**.

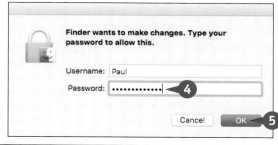

A OS X uninstalls the application.

TIP

Is there another way to uninstall an application?
Yes, in some cases. A few Mac applications come with a separate program for uninstalling the application:

1 Follow steps **1** and **2**.

2 Open the application's folder, if it has one.

Note: Some programs store their uninstallers in Utilities, which is a subfolder of Applications.

3 Double-click the **Uninstall** (or **Uninstaller**) icon and then follow the instructions on-screen.

Force a Stuck Application to Close

When you are working with an application, you may find that it becomes unresponsive and you cannot interact with the application or even quit the application normally. In that case, you can use an OS X feature called Force Quit to force a stuck or unresponsive application to close, which enables you to restart the application or restart your Mac.

Unfortunately, when you force an application to quit, you lose any unsaved changes in that application's open documents. Therefore, you should make sure the application really is stuck before forcing it to quit. See the second Tip for more information.

Force a Stuck Application to Close

1 Click **Apple** (🍎).

2 Click **Force Quit**.

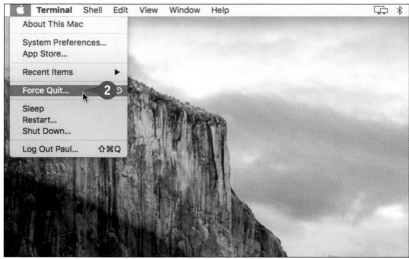

The Force Quit Applications window appears.

③ Click the application you want to shut down.

④ Click **Force Quit**.

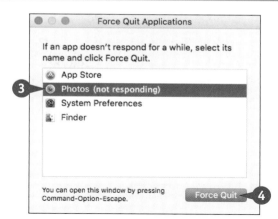

Your Mac asks you to confirm that you want to force the application to quit.

⑤ Click **Force Quit**.

Your Mac shuts down the application.

⑥ Click **Close** (⬤) to close the Force Quit Applications window.

Are there easier ways to run the Force Quit command?

Yes. From the keyboard, you can run the Force Quit command by pressing `Option`+`⌘`+`Esc`. If the application has a Dock icon, press and hold `Control`+`Option`, click the application's Dock icon, and then click **Force Quit**.

If an application is not responding, does that always mean the application is stuck?

Not necessarily. Some operations — such as recalculating a large spreadsheet or rendering a 3-D image — can take a few minutes, and the application can appear stuck. Low memory can also cause an application to seem stuck. In this case, try shutting down applications to free some memory.

Configure Time Machine Backups

One of the most crucial OS X maintenance chores is to configure your system to make regular backups of your files. Macs are reliable machines, but they can crash and all hard drives eventually die, so at some point your data will be at risk. To avoid losing that data forever, you need to configure Time Machine to perform regular backups.

To use Time Machine, your Mac requires a second hard drive. This can be a second internal drive on a Mac mini, but on most Macs the easiest course is to connect an external hard drive.

Configure Time Machine Backups

1. Connect an external USB, Thunderbolt, or FireWire hard drive to your Mac.

   If OS X asks if you want to use the hard drive as your backup disk, click **Use as Backup Disk** and then skip the rest of these steps.

2. Click **System Preferences** (⚙).

   The System Preferences appear.

3. Click **Time Machine**.

   The Time Machine preferences appear.

4. Click **Select Backup Disk**.

Time Machine displays a list of available backup devices.

5 Click the external hard drive.

6 Click **Use Disk**.

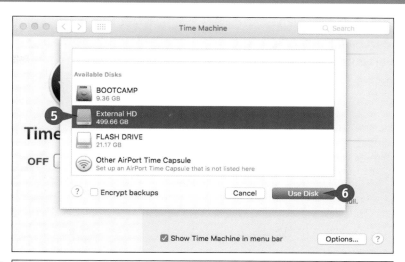

A Time Machine enables backups and prepares to run the first backup automatically in 2 minutes.

7 Click **Close** (●).

TIP

How do Time Machine backups work?

Time Machine backups are handled automatically as follows:

- The initial backup occurs 2 minutes after you configure Time Machine for the first time. This backup includes your entire Mac.
- Another backup runs every hour. These hourly backups include files and folders you have changed or created since the most recent hourly backup.
- Time Machine runs a daily backup that includes only those files and folders that you have changed or created since the most recent daily backup.
- Time Machine runs a weekly backup that includes only those files and folders that you have changed or created since the most recent weekly backup.

Restore an Earlier Version of a File

If you improperly edit or accidentally overwrite a file, some apps enable you to revert to an earlier version of the file. Why would you want to revert to an earlier version of a file? One reason is that you might improperly edit the file by deleting or changing important data. In some cases, you may be able to restore that data by going back to a previous version of the file. Similarly, if you overwrite the file with a different file, you can fix the problem by restoring an earlier version of the file.

Restore an Earlier Version of a File

1 Open the file you want to restore.

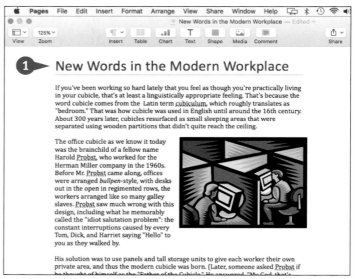

2 Click **File**.

3 Click **Revert To**.

Note: If you do not see the Revert To command, it means the application does not support this feature.

Ⓐ To restore the most recently saved version, click **Last Saved**.

Ⓑ To restore the most recently opened version, click **Last Opened**.

4 Click **Browse All Versions**.

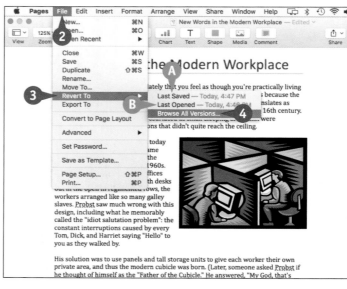

The restore interface appears.

C This window represents the current version of the file.

D Each of these windows represents an earlier version of the file.

E This area tells you when the displayed version of the file was saved.

F You can use this timeline to navigate the earlier versions.

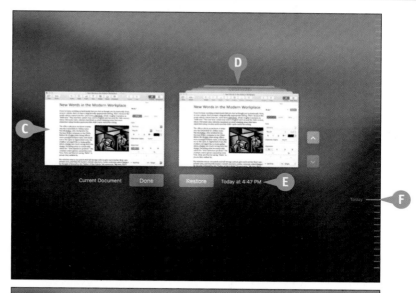

5 Navigate to the date that contains the version of the file you want to restore.

Note: See the first Tip to learn how to navigate the Time Machine backups.

6 Click **Restore**.

OS X reverts the file to the earlier version.

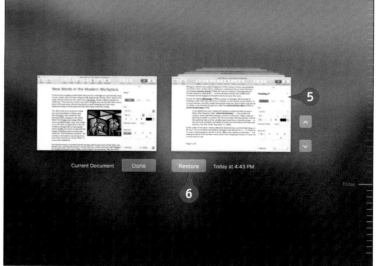

TIPS

How do I navigate the previous versions?
There are two methods you can use:

- Use the timeline on the right side of the window to click a specific version.

- Click the title bars of the version windows.

Can I restore a previous version without overwriting the current version of the file?
Yes, you can restore a copy of the file. This is useful if the current version has data you want to preserve, or if you want to compare the two versions. Follow steps **1** to **5** to navigate to the version you want to restore. Press and hold Option, and then click **Restore a Copy**.

Restore Files Using Time Machine

If you have configured OS X to make regular Time Machine backups, you can use those backups to restore a lost file. If you accidentally delete a file, you can quickly restore it by opening the Trash folder. However, that does not help you if you have emptied the Trash folder. Similarly, if the program or OS X crashes, a file may become corrupted.

Because Time Machine makes hourly, daily, and weekly backups, it stores older copies of your data. You can use these backups to restore any file that you accidentally delete or that has become corrupted.

Restore Files Using Time Machine

1 Click **Finder** ( ).

2 Open the folder you want to restore, or the folder that contains the file you want to restore.

Note: If you have repaired or replaced your original hard drive, you can restore the entire drive by pressing **Shift**+**⌘**+**C** and then double-clicking the drive (usually **Macintosh HD**).

3 Click **Spotlight** ( ).

4 Type **time machine**.

5 Double-click **Time Machine**.

The Time Machine interface appears.

A Each window represents a backed-up version of the folder.

B This area tells you when the displayed version of the folder was backed up.

C You can use this timeline to navigate the backed-up versions.

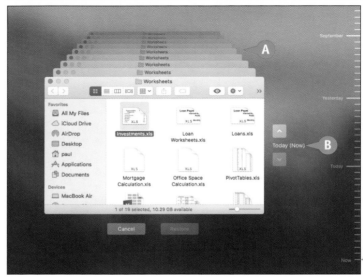

6 Navigate to the date that contains the backed-up version of the folder or file.

Note: See the Tip to learn how to navigate the Time Machine backups.

7 If you are restoring a file, click the file.

8 Click **Restore**.

If another version of the folder or file already exists, Time Machine asks if you want to keep it or replace it.

9 Click **Replace**.

Time Machine restores the folder or file.

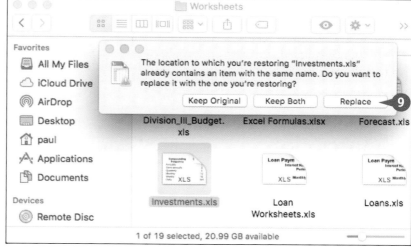

How do I navigate the backups in the Time Machine interface?

Here are the most useful techniques:

- Click the top arrow to jump to the earliest version; click the bottom arrow to return to the most recent version.
- Press and hold ⌘ and click the arrows to navigate through the backups one version at a time.
- Use the timeline to click a specific version.
- Click the version windows.

Recondition Your Mac Notebook Battery

To get the most performance out of your Mac notebook's battery, you need to recondition the battery by cycling it. *Cycling* a battery means letting it completely discharge and then fully recharging it again. Most Mac notebook batteries slowly lose their charging capacity over time. For example, if you can use your Mac notebook on batteries for 4 hours today, later on you will only be able to run the computer for 3 hours on a full charge. You cannot stop this process, but you can delay it significantly by cycling the battery once a month or so.

Recondition Your Mac Notebook Battery

Display the Battery Status Percentage

1. Click **Battery Status** (⊞).

2. Click **Show Percentage**.

   Your Mac shows the percentage of available battery power remaining.

Cycle the Battery

1. Disconnect your Mac notebook's power cord.

ⓐ The Battery Status icon changes from ⊞ to ▬.

2 Operate your Mac notebook normally by running applications, working with documents, and so on.

3 As you work, keep your eye on the battery status percentage.

When the battery status reaches 8% the meter turns red, and when the status reaches 5%, OS X warns you that the system will soon go into sleep mode.

4 Click **Close**.

5 Reattach the power cord.

Your Mac restarts and the Battery Status icon changes from 🔋 to ⚡.

6 Leave your Mac plugged in at least until the battery status shows 100%.

TIP

I do not see the battery status in my menu bar. How do I display it?
Click **System Preferences** (⚙) in the Dock to open System Preferences, and then click **Energy Saver**. In the Energy Saver window, click the **Show battery status in menu bar** check box (☐ changes to ☑). Click **Close** (⬤).

Restart Your Mac

If an application is behaving erratically or if a device attached to your Mac stops working, it often helps to restart your Mac. By rebooting the computer, you reload the entire system, which is often enough to solve many computer problems.

For a device that gets power from the Mac, such as some external hard drives, restarting your Mac might not resolve the problem because the device remains powered up the whole time. You can *power cycle* — shut down and then restart — such devices as a group by power cycling your Mac.

Restart Your Mac

Restart Your Mac

1 Click **Apple** (🍎).

2 Click **Restart**.

Your Mac asks you to confirm.

3 Click **Restart**.

Note: To bypass the confirmation dialog, press and hold **Option** when you click the **Restart** command.

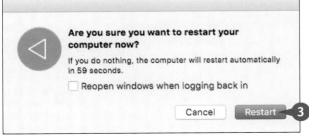

Power Cycle Your Mac

1 Click **Apple** ().

2 Click **Shut Down**.

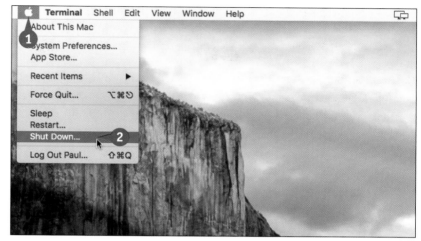

Your Mac asks you to confirm.

Note: To bypass the confirmation dialog, press and hold Option when you click **Shut Down**.

3 Click **Shut Down**.

4 Wait for 30 seconds to give all devices time to spin down.

5 Turn your Mac back on.

TIP

What other basic troubleshooting techniques can I use?

• Make sure that each device is turned on, that cable connections are secure, and that insertable devices (such as USB devices) are properly inserted.

• If a device is battery-powered, replace the batteries.

• If a device has an on/off switch, power cycle the device by turning it off, waiting a few seconds for it to stop spinning, and then turning it back on again.

• Close all running programs.

• Log out of your Mac — click **Apple** (); click **Log Out** *User*, where *User* is your Mac username; and then click **Log Out** — and then log back in again.

CHAPTER 14

Working with iCloud

You can get a free iCloud account, which is an online service that lets you automatically synchronize data between iCloud and your Mac (as well as your iPhone, iPad, or iPod touch). You can also use iCloud to generate website passwords, store documents online, and locate a lost Mac.

Create an Apple ID

To use iCloud, you need to create a free Apple ID, which you use to sign in to iCloud on the web and to synchronize your Mac and other devices. An Apple ID is an email address. You can use an existing email address for your Apple ID. When you use an existing email address, you are required to verify via email that the address is legitimate. Once you have created an Apple ID, you can use it to sign in to iCloud on the web, on your Mac, and on your devices, such as your iPhone or iPad.

Create an Apple ID

1 Click **System Preferences** (⚙).

The System Preferences appear.

2 Click **iCloud**.

The iCloud preferences appear.

3 Click **Create Apple ID**.

The Create an Apple ID dialog appears.

④ Click the **Location** ⬦ to choose your country.

⑤ Click the three **Birthday** pop-up menus to choose your month, day, and year of birth.

⑥ Click **Continue**.

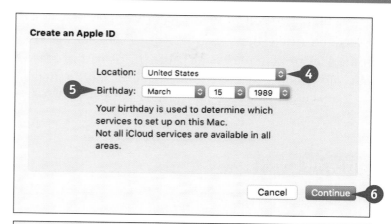

⑦ Type your name.

⑧ Type the email address you want to use.

⑨ Type the password (twice).

⑩ Click **Continue**.

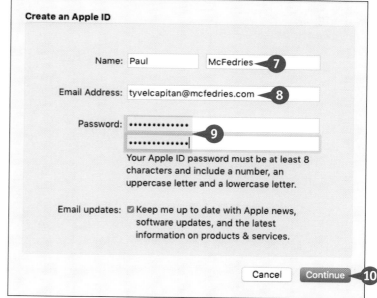

TIP

iCloud does not accept my password. Why?
Apple has fairly stringent requirements when it comes to the passwords used for iCloud accounts. First, the entire password must be at least eight characters long. Anything less and Apple rejects it. Also, the password must include at least one character from each of the following three sets: lowercase letters, uppercase letters, and numbers. If you do not use at least one character from all those sets, Apple will reject your password. Finally, spaces are not allowed, so make sure you are not including any spaces in your password.

continued ▶

Create an Apple ID (continued)

Although there is nothing to stop you from using any email address as your Apple ID, you really should use an address that belongs to you. Also, you need to be able to retrieve and read messages that are sent to that address, because this is part of the verification process. That is, once you give Apple your details and agree to the terms of service, Apple will send a verification message to the email address you provided. Before you can use your iCloud account, you must click a verification link in that message.

Create an Apple ID (continued)

⑪ For each security question, click ⬍ to select a question and then type an answer.

⑫ Click **Continue**.

⑬ Click **Agree**.

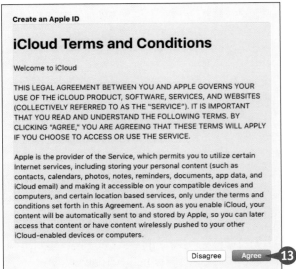

Apple sends an email message to the address you typed in step **8**.

14 In your email program, open the message from Apple.

15 Click **Verify now**.

Apple prompts you to sign in to verify your email address.

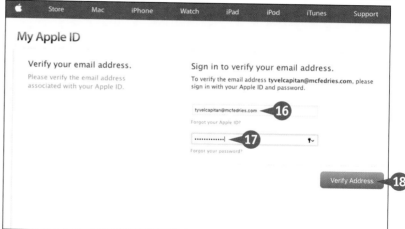

16 Type your Apple ID (that is, the email address from step **8**).

17 Type your password.

18 Click **Verify Address**.

Apple verifies your address and then OS X sets up your iCloud account on your Mac.

TIP

Why do I not see any iCloud data on my Mac?

At this point, you have verified your address and OS X has set up your new iCloud account on your Mac. However, OS X does not synchronize any iCloud data automatically. Instead, you need to sign in to iCloud on your Mac and then choose which services you want to synchronize between your Mac and iCloud. See the section "Set Up iCloud Synchronization," later in this chapter, for details.

Sign In to iCloud Online

Although you can access most iCloud features using your Mac, you can also sign in online using a web browser, which is useful if you need to access iCloud data when using someone else's Mac or Windows PC. Most modern browsers work well with iCloud, but Apple recommends that you use at least Safari 8, Firefox 22, Internet Explorer 10, or Chrome 28.

To sign in to iCloud using a Mac, you must be using at least OS X Lion 10.7.5, although Apple recommends OS X Yosemite (10.10.3) or later. To access iCloud using a Windows PC, the PC must be running Windows 7 or later.

Sign In to iCloud Online

1 In your web browser, type www.icloud.com.

2 Press **Return**.

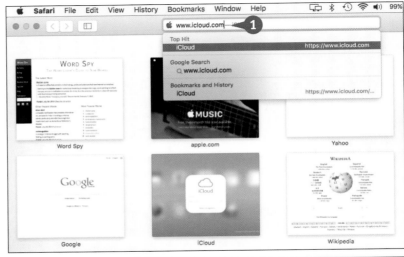

The iCloud Login page appears.

3 Type your Apple ID in the Apple ID text box.

4 Type the password for your Apple ID in the Password text box.

Ⓐ If you want iCloud to sign you in automatically in the future, click the **Keep me signed in** check box (changes to ✓).

⑤ Click **Sign In** (→).

The first time you sign in, iCloud prompts you to configure some settings.

⑥ Click **Add Photo**, drop a photo on the dialog that appears, and then click **Done**.

⑦ Click **Start Using iCloud.**

TIPS

Can I sign in from my Mac?
Yes. Click **System Preferences** (◉) in the Dock (or click and then click **System Preferences**) and then click **iCloud**. Type your Apple ID and password and then click **Sign In**.

How do I sign out from iCloud?
When you are done working with your iCloud account, if you prefer not to remain signed in to your account, click your account name in the upper right corner of the iCloud page and then click **Sign Out**.

Set Up iCloud Synchronization

Y ou can ensure that your Mac and your iCloud account have the same data by synchronizing the two. The main items you will want to synchronize are email accounts, contacts, calendars, reminders, and notes. However, there are many other types of data you may want to synchronize to iCloud, including Safari bookmarks, photos, and documents. If you have a second Mac, a Windows PC, or an iPhone, iPad, or iPod touch, you can also synchronize it with the same iCloud account, which ensures that your Mac and the device use the same data.

Set Up iCloud Synchronization

① Click **System Preferences** (⚙).

The System Preferences appear.

② Click **iCloud**.

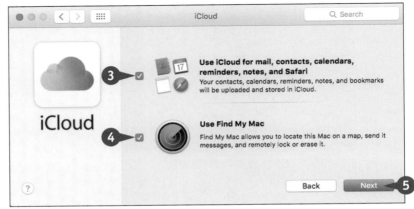

The first time you open iCloud, OS X prompts you to choose which iCloud services you want to use.

③ If you do not want to sync your data to iCloud, click the **Use iCloud for mail, contacts, calendars, reminders, notes, and Safari** check box (☑ changes to ☐).

④ If you do not want to use iCloud to locate your Mac, click the **Use Find My Mac** check box (☑ changes to ☐).

⑤ Click **Next**.

If you elected to use Find My Mac, OS X asks you to confirm.

6 Click **Allow**.

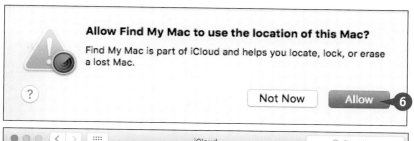

Allow Find My Mac to use the location of this Mac?

Find My Mac is part of iCloud and helps you locate, lock, or erase a lost Mac.

Not Now   Allow **6**

The iCloud preferences appear.

7 Click the check box beside a type of data you want to sync (☐ changes to ✓).

Note: If you do not want to sync a type of data, click its check box (✓ changes to ☐). If OS X asks if you want to keep or delete the iCloud data that you are no longer syncing, click **Keep** or click **Delete from Mac**.

Your Mac synchronizes the data with your iCloud account.

Paul McFedries
paulmcfedries@mac.com

Account Details

Set Up Family

iCloud   Q Search

☑ iCloud Drive

☐ Photos   Options...

☑ Mail

☑ Contacts **7**

☑ Calendars

☑ Reminders

☑ Safari

☑ Notes

You have 25 GB of iCloud storage.

Sign Out   18.37 GB Available   Manage...

TIP

What happens if I modify an appointment, contact, bookmark, or other data in iCloud?
The synchronization process works both ways. That is, all the Mac data you selected to synchronize is sent to your iCloud account. However, the data on your iCloud account is also sent to your Mac. This means that if you modify, add, or delete data on your iCloud account, those changes are also reflected in your Mac's copies.

Set Up iCloud Keychain

You can make it easier to navigate secure websites by setting up iCloud Keychain. A *keychain* is a master list of usernames and passwords that a system stores for easy access by an authorized user. iCloud Keychain is a special type of keychain that stores website passwords auto-generated by Safari, as described in the next section, "Generate a Website Password." This means that you do not have to remember these passwords because Safari can automatically retrieve them from your iCloud account.

Set Up iCloud Keychain

1 Click **System Preferences** (⚙).

The System Preferences appear.

2 Click **iCloud**.

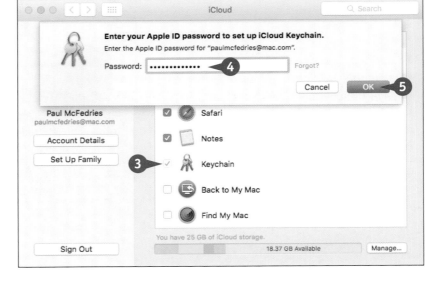

The iCloud preferences appear.

3 Click the **Keychain** check box
(☐ changes to ☑).

Note: If OS X prompts you to create a password to unlock your screen, see Chapter 11.

OS X prompts you for your Apple ID password.

4 Type your password.

5 Click **OK**.

OS X prompts you to enter an iCloud security code.

6 Type a six-digit security code.

7 Click **Next**.

OS X prompts you to confirm the iCloud security code.

8 Repeat steps **6** and **7** to confirm the security code.

OS X prompts you to enter a phone number that can receive SMS (text) messages.

Note: If you have previously set up a phone number with iCloud, OS X sends a verification code to that number and then prompts you to enter the code.

9 Type the phone number.

10 Click **Done**.

OS X activates iCloud Keychain.

Create an iCloud Security Code.
Your iCloud Security Code can be used to set up iCloud Keychain on a new device.

6

Enter a six-digit numeric security code.

Advanced...   Cancel   Next **7**

Enter a phone number that can receive SMS messages:

Country: +1 (Canada)

Number: (317) 555-2468 **9**

This number will be used to verify your identity when using your iCloud Security Code. This can be your own number, or the number of someone you trust.

Cancel   Done **10**

TIPS

Can I use iCloud Keychain only on my Mac?
No, *any* Mac or iOS device such as an iPhone or iPad that uses the same iCloud account has access to the same keychain, so your saved website passwords also work on those devices. On the downside, this sets up a possible security problem should you lose your iPhone or iPad. Therefore, be sure to configure your device with a passcode lock to prevent unauthorized access to your iCloud Keychain.

How do I change my security code or verification phone number?
If you want to use a different security code, or if the phone number you use for verification has changed, you should update these important security features as soon as possible. Display the iCloud preferences and then click **Options** beside Keychain.

Generate a Website Password

You can make it easier and faster to navigate many websites by using Safari to generate, and iCloud to store, passwords for those sites that require you to log in. Many websites require you to set up an account, which means you must log in with a username and password. Good security practices dictate using a unique and hard-to-guess password for each site, but this requires memorizing a large number of passwords. To enhance security and ease web navigation, you can use Safari to automatically generate for each site a unique and secure password stored safely with your iCloud account.

Generate a Website Password

Generate a Website Password

1 Turn on iCloud Keychain.

Note: See the previous section, "Set Up iCloud Keychain," to learn how to activate iCloud Keychain.

2 In Safari, navigate to a web page that requires a new password.

3 Click inside the password field.

A Safari displays its suggested password.

4 Click the password.

B iCloud enters the password. iCloud also enters the password in the confirmation field, if one exists.

5 Fill in the rest of the website form data as required.

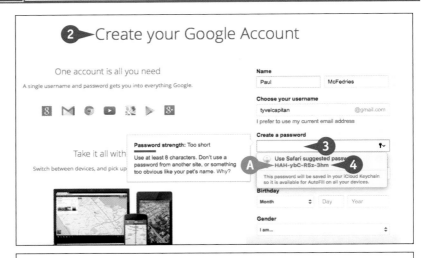

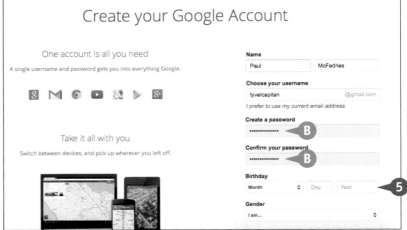

Using a Generated Website Password

1 In Safari, navigate to a web page that requires you to log in using a previously generated password.

2 Click inside the Password box.

3 Click **Keychain** (🔑︎).

4 Click the saved website password.

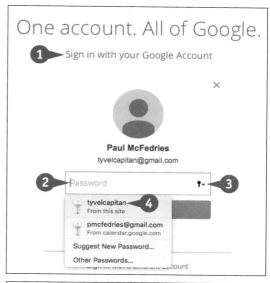

C Safari fills in the website password.

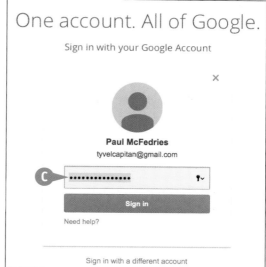

TIP

How do I get access to website passwords on another device?

You must activate iCloud Keychain on the other device and then authorize the other device to use the keychain. When you activate iCloud Keychain — see the previous section — iCloud gives you two ways to continue. As a first option, if a device that has previously been authorized to use your iCloud Keychain is available, click **Request Approval**. On the other device, click **Allow**. As a second option, if a device that has previously been authorized to use your iCloud Keychain is not available, click **Use Code**, type your six-digit iCloud security code, click **Next**, and then enter the verification code that iCloud sends via text message.

Activate and Configure iCloud Drive

You can use the iCloud Drive feature to store documents online. You can then access those documents either via the iCloud website or by using any other device — such as an iPhone or iPad — that is signed in to the same iCloud account. iCloud Drive works with all your Mac apps, so you can store any document in any iCloud Drive folder. If you have apps that you do not want to access your online storage, you can configure iCloud Drive to exclude those apps.

Activate and Configure iCloud Drive

1 Click **System Preferences** (⚙).

The System Preferences appear.

2 Click **iCloud**.

The iCloud preferences appear.

3 Click the **iCloud Drive** check box (☐ changes to ☑).

OS X activates iCloud Drive on your Mac.

4 Click **Options**.

5 Click the **Documents** tab.

OS X displays a list of apps that store documents using iCloud Drive.

6 Click the check box for each app that you do not want to access iCloud Drive (☑ changes to ☐).

7 Click **Done**.

8 Click **Close** (●).

OS X puts your iCloud Drive settings into effect.

TIP

How do apps store documents using iCloud Drive?
It depends on the app. In some cases, an app is given its own iCloud Drive folder, which is a special storage area called an *application library*. Apps that get their own folders on iCloud Drive include TextEdit, Preview, Pages, Numbers, and Keynote. For all other apps, as well as apps that have their own libraries, you can store documents either in the main iCloud Drive folder or in a subfolder.

Save and Open Documents Using iCloud Drive

Now that you have activated iCloud Drive, you can use any OS X application to save your documents to iCloud Drive. If a program has its own iCloud Drive application library, you can use that folder to save your documents. Otherwise, you can save your documents in any iCloud Drive folder.

Once you have documents saved to iCloud Drive, you can use the associated OS X applications to open and work with those documents. You can also access iCloud Drive documents directly using Finder.

Save and Open Documents Using iCloud Drive

Save to an Application Library

1. Run the app's Save command.

Note: In most apps, you run the Save command by clicking **File** and then clicking **Save**, or by pressing ⌘+S.

2. Click the **Where** ⬦ and then click *App* — **iCloud**, where *App* is the name of the app, such as Pages, as shown here.

3. Fill in the other file details.

4. Click **Save**.

OS X saves the document to the program's application library.

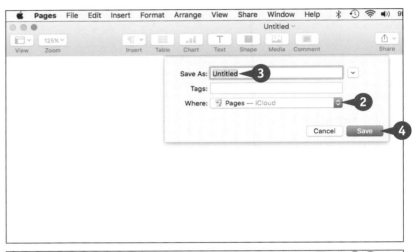

Save to Any iCloud Drive Folder

1. Run the app's Save command.

2. Click **Expand** (⌄).

OS X expands the dialog.

③ In the Favorites section of the sidebar, click **iCloud Drive**.

OS X displays the contents of your main iCloud Drive folder.

④ Double-click the folder you want to use to store the document.

⑤ Fill in the other file details.

⑥ Click **Save**.

OS X saves the document to the iCloud Drive folder.

Open a Document Using Finder

① Click **Finder** ( ).

② In the sidebar's Favorites section, click **iCloud Drive**.

③ Open the folder than contains the document you want to open.

④ Double-click the document.

OS X opens the document in its associated application.

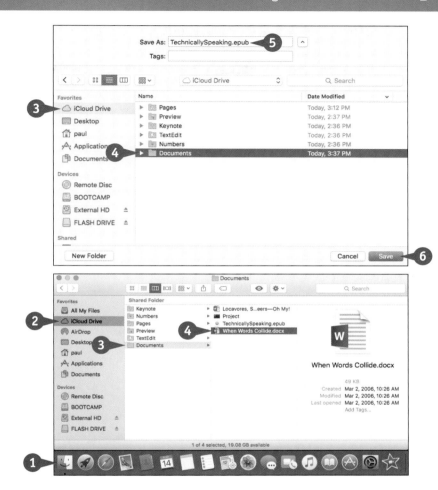

Manage Your iCloud Storage

The iCloud preferences include a feature that enables you to manage your iCloud Drive storage. When you sign up for iCloud, Apple automatically gives you 5GB of free storage. Upgrading your storage, as described in the Tip at the end of this section, costs money, so if you do not want to spend anything for your iCloud Drive storage, then you need to manage your storage. This means deleting data that you no longer need from iCloud Drive. You can delete the backups stored for one or more devices, or you can delete the documents and data stored by one or more apps.

Manage Your iCloud Storage

1 Click **System Preferences** (⚙).

The System Preferences appear.

2 Click **iCloud**.

The iCloud preferences appear.

3 Click **Manage**.

The Manage Storage dialog appears.

④ Click **Backups**.

⑤ Click the device backup you want to remove.

⑥ Click **Delete**.

iCloud Drive asks you to confirm.

⑦ Click **Delete**.

iCloud Drive removes the device backup.

⑧ Click an app.

⑨ Click **Delete Documents and Data**.

iCloud Drive asks you to confirm.

⑩ Click **Delete**.

⑪ Repeat steps **8** to **10** to remove the data for other apps, as needed.

⑫ Click **Done**.

⑬ Click **Close** (●).

OS X puts your iCloud Drive settings into effect.

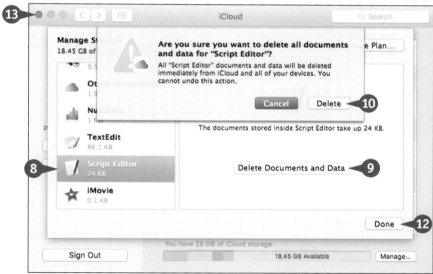

TIP

How do I change my iCloud storage plan?

iCloud Drive comes with 5GB of online file storage. If you are getting low on iCloud Drive storage space, then you should consider upgrading your storage plan to give yourself more room. You can get 50GB for $0.99 a month, 200GB for $2.99 a month, or 1TB for $9.99 a month. To upgrade your plan, follow steps **1** to **3** to open the Manage Storage dialog, and then click **Change Storage Plan**. The Upgrade iCloud Storage dialog appears. Click the storage plan you want to use, click **Next**, type your Apple ID password, and then click **Buy**.

Set Up Family Sharing

Not being able to see what other members of your family are sharing on iCloud has long been a major drawback of the service because the only way to work around it was to share an account. Now, however, iCloud offers a feature called Family Sharing, which lets up to six family members share each other's content, including photos, calendars, and reminders. And if purchases are made through the App Store, iTunes Store, or iBookstore using a single credit card, then each family member also gets access to the others' purchased apps, songs, movies, TV shows, and e-books, where the seller allows that sharing.

Set Up Family Sharing

Note: These steps assume you want to be the Family Sharing organizer, which means you are responsible for maintaining Family Sharing.

1 Click **System Preferences** (⚙) in the Dock (not shown).

2 Click **iCloud** (not shown).

The iCloud preferences appear.

3 Click **Set Up Family**.

The Family Sharing preferences appear.

4 Click **Continue**.

iCloud asks if you want to be the organizer.

5 Click **Continue**.

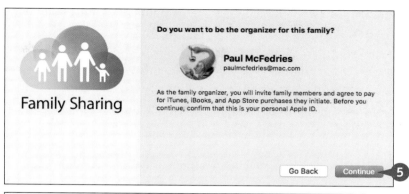

iCloud lets you know that purchases made through your account will be shared with your family.

6 Click **Continue**.

iCloud displays the payment method associated with your account.

7 Click **Continue**.

iCloud asks if you want to share your location with your family.

8 Click the **Share your location** option (○ changes to ●) (not shown).

9 Click **Continue** (not shown).

iCloud sets up Family Sharing.

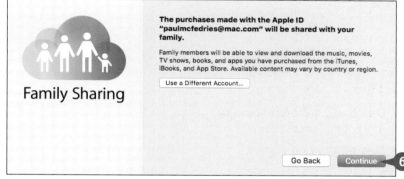

TIP

How do I add family members?
When you complete the Family Sharing setup, iCloud displays the Manage Family Sharing dialog. You can also display this dialog at any time by clicking **Manage Family** in the iCloud preferences. Click **Add Family Member** (✚), enter the person's name or email address, and then click **Continue**. Click the **Ask this family member to enter the password** option (○ changes to ●) and then type the password for that person's iCloud account. If you do not know the password, click **Send *Name* an invitation**, instead (where *Name* is the family member's name). Click **Continue**.

Locate and Lock a Lost Mac, iPod, iPhone, or iPad

You can use iCloud to locate a lost or stolen Mac, iPod touch, iPhone, or iPad. Depending on how you use your Mac, iPod touch, iPhone, or iPad, you can end up with many details of your life residing on the device. That is generally a good thing, but if you happen to lose your device, you have also lost those details, plus you have created a large privacy problem because anyone can now see your data. You can locate your device and even remotely lock the device using an iCloud feature called Find My iPhone, which also works for Macs, iPod touches, and iPads.

Locate and Lock a Lost Mac, iPod, iPhone, or iPad

1 Sign in to the iCloud website.

Note: See the section "Sign In to iCloud Online," earlier in this chapter.

2 Click **Find My iPhone**.

Note: If iCloud asks you to sign in to your account, type your password and click **Sign In**.

3 Click **All Devices**.

4 Click the device you want to locate.

A iCloud displays the device location on a map.

5 Click **Lost Mode**.

The Lost Mode dialog appears. If the device is not protected by a passcode, iCloud prompts you to enter one. If the device is protected by a passcode, you can skip to step **8**.

6 Type a four-digit lock code.

7 Type the lock code again to confirm (not shown).

iCloud prompts you to enter a phone number where you can be contacted.

8 Type the phone number.

9 Click **Next**.

iCloud prompts you to enter a message to display on the device.

10 Type your message.

11 Click **Done**.

iCloud locks the device and sends the message, which then appears on the device screen.

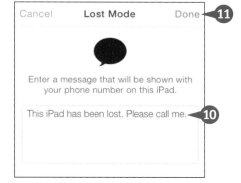

TIP

I tried to enable Find My Mac, but OS X would not allow it. How can I enable Find My Mac?
You first need to enable location services. To do this, click **System Preferences** (⚙) in the Dock. In the System Preferences, click **Security & Privacy**, click the lock icon (🔒), type your OS X administrator password, and then click **OK** (🔒 changes to 🔓). Click **Privacy**, click **Location Services**, and then click the **Enable Location Services** check box (☐ changes to ☑).

CHAPTER 15

Networking with OS X

If you have multiple computers in your home or office, you can set up these computers as a network to share information and equipment. This chapter gives an overview of networking concepts and shows you how to connect to a network, how to work with the other computers on your network, and how to share your Mac's resources with other network users.

Understanding Networking

A *network* is a collection of computers and other devices that are connected. You can create a network using cable hookups, wireless hookups, or a combination of the two. In both cases, you need special networking equipment to make the connections.

A network gives you a number of advantages. For example, once you have two or more computers connected on a network, those computers can share documents, photos, and other files. You can also use a network to share equipment, such as printers and optical drives.

Shared Resources

Share Files

Networked computers are connected to each other, and so they can exchange files with each other along the connection. This enables people to share information and to collaborate on projects. OS X includes built-in security, so that you can control what files you share with other people.

Share Equipment

Computers connected over a network can share some types of equipment. For example, one computer can share its printer, which enables other network users to send their documents to that printer. Networked computers can also share hard drives, optical drives, and document scanners.

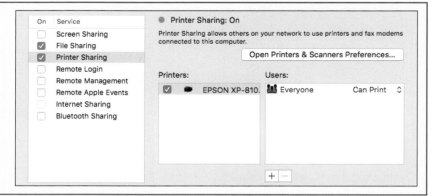

Wired Networking

Network Cable

A *network cable* is a special cable designed for exchanging information. One end of the cable plugs into the Mac's network port, if it has one. The other end plugs into a network connection point, which is usually the network's router (discussed next), but it could also be a switch, hub, or even another Mac. Information, shared files, and other network data travel through the network cables.

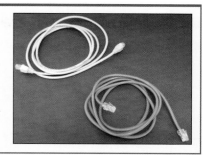

Router

A *router* is a central connection point for all the computers on the wired portion of the network. For each computer, you run a network cable from the Mac's network port to a port in the router. When network data travels from computer A to computer B, it first goes out through computer A's network port, along its network cable, and into the router. Then the router passes the data along computer B's network cable and into its network port.

Wireless Networking

Wireless Connections

A *wireless network* is a collection of two or more computers that communicate with each other using radio signals instead of cable. The most common wireless technology is Wi-Fi (rhymes with hi-fi) or 802.11. Each of the four main types (802.11ac, 802.11b, 802.11g, and 802.11n) has its own range and speed limits. The other common wireless technology is Bluetooth, which enables devices to communicate directly with each other.

Wireless Router

A *wireless router* is a device that receives and transmits signals from wireless computers to form a wireless network. Many wireless routers also accept wired connections, which enables both wired and wireless computers to form a network. If your network has a broadband modem, you can connect the modem to your wireless router to extend Internet access to all the computers on the network.

Connect a Bluetooth Device

You can make wireless connections to devices such as mice, keyboards, headsets, and cell phones by using the Bluetooth networking technology. The networking tasks that you learn about in the rest of this chapter require special equipment to connect your computers and devices. However, with Bluetooth devices, the networking is built in, so no extra equipment is needed. For Bluetooth connections to work, your device must be Bluetooth-enabled and your Mac and the Bluetooth device must remain within about 30 feet of each other.

Connect a Bluetooth Device

Connect a Bluetooth Device Without a Passkey

1 Click **System Preferences** (⚙) in the Dock.

2 Click **Bluetooth**.

The Bluetooth preferences appear.

3 Click **Turn Bluetooth On**.

OS X activates Bluetooth and makes your Mac discoverable.

④ Perform whatever steps are necessary to make your Bluetooth device discoverable.

Note: For example, if you are connecting a Bluetooth mouse, the device often has a separate switch or button that makes the mouse discoverable, so you need to turn on that switch or press that button.

Ⓐ A list of the available Bluetooth devices appears here.

⑤ Click **Pair** beside the Bluetooth device you want to connect.

⑥ Perform the steps required to pair your Mac and your device.

Ⓑ Your Mac connects with the device.

TIPS

What does it mean to make a device discoverable?
This means that you configure the device to broadcast that it is available for a Bluetooth connection. Controlling the broadcast is important because you usually want to use a Bluetooth device such as a mouse or keyboard with only a single computer.

What does pairing mean?
As a security precaution, many Bluetooth devices do not connect automatically to other devices. Otherwise, a stranger with a Bluetooth device could connect to your cell phone or even your Mac. To prevent this, most Bluetooth devices require you to type a password before the connection is made. This is known as *pairing* the two devices.

continued ▶

A Bluetooth mouse and a Bluetooth headset do not require any extra pairing steps, although with a headset you must configure OS X to use it for sound output. However, pairing devices such as a Bluetooth keyboard and a Bluetooth cell phone does require an extra step. In most cases, pairing is accomplished by your Mac generating a 6- or 8-digit *passkey* that you must then type into the Bluetooth device (assuming that it has some kind of keypad). In other cases, the device comes with a default passkey that you must type into your Mac to set up the pairing.

Connect a Bluetooth Device (continued)

Connect a Bluetooth Device with a Passkey

1 Turn the device on, if required.

2 Turn on the switch that makes the device discoverable, if required.

3 Follow steps 1 and 2 in the subsection "Connect a Bluetooth Device Without a Passkey" to display a list of available Bluetooth devices.

4 Click **Pair** beside your Bluetooth device.

The Bluetooth Setup Assistant displays a passkey.

5 Use the Bluetooth device to type the displayed passkey.

6 Press **Return**.

OS X connects to the device. If you see the Keyboard Setup Assistant, follow the on-screen instructions to set up the keyboard for use with your Mac.

Listen to Audio Through Bluetooth Headphones

1 Click **System Preferences** (⊚) in the Dock.

2 Click **Sound**.

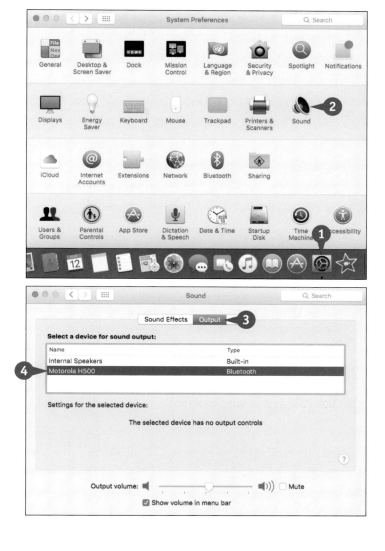

The Sound preferences appear.

3 Click the **Output** tab.

4 Click the Bluetooth headphones.

How do I remove a Bluetooth device?
To remove a Bluetooth device, first follow steps **1** and **2** in the subsection "Connect a Bluetooth Device Without a Passkey." Position the mouse (⬆) over the device you want to disconnect and then click **Disconnect** (✕) (Ⓐ). When OS X asks you to confirm, click **Remove**. OS X removes the device.

Connect to a Wireless Network

All the latest Macs have built-in wireless networking capability that you can use to connect to a wireless network that is within range. This could be a network in your home, your office, or a public location such as a coffee shop. In most cases, this also gives you access to the wireless network's Internet connection.

Most wireless networks have security turned on, which means you must know the correct password to connect to the network. However, after you connect to the network once, your Mac remembers the password and connects automatically the next time the network comes within range.

Connect to a Wireless Network

① Click **Wi-Fi status** (🛜) in the menu bar.

Your Mac locates the wireless networks within range of your Mac.

Ⓐ The available networks appear in the menu.

Ⓑ Networks with a lock icon (🔒) require a password to join.

② Click the wireless network you want to join.

If the wireless network is secure, your Mac prompts you for the password.

③ Type the network password in the Password text box.

C If the password is very long and you are sure no one can see your screen, you can click the **Show password** check box (☐ changes to ☑) to see the actual characters rather than dots. This helps to ensure you type the password correctly.

④ Click **Join**.

Your Mac connects to the wireless network.

D The Wi-Fi status icon changes from 🛜 to 🛜 to indicate the connection.

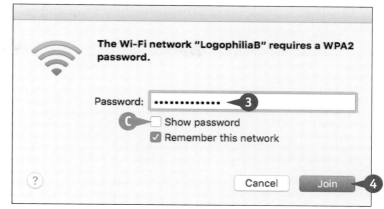

TIPS

I know a particular network is within range, but I do not see it in the list. Why not?
As a security precaution, some wireless networks do not broadcast their availability. However, you can still connect to such a network, assuming you know its name and the password. Click **Wi-Fi status** (🛜) and then click **Join Other Network**.

I do not see the Wi-Fi status icon on my menu bar. How do I display the icon?
Click **System Preferences** (⚙) to open the System Preferences. Click **Network**, click **Wi-Fi**, and then click the **Show Wi-Fi status in menu bar** check box (☐ changes to ☑).

Connect to a Network Resource

To see what other network users have shared on the network, you can use the Network folder to view the other computers and then connect to them to see their shared resources. To get full access to a Mac's shared resources, you must connect with a username and password for an administrator account on that Mac. To get access to the resources that have been shared by a particular user, you must connect with that user's name and password. Note, too, that your Mac can also connect to the resources shared by Windows computers.

Connect to a Network Resource

1 Click the desktop.

2 Click **Go**.

3 Click **Network**.

Note: Another way to run the Network command is to press Shift+⌘+K.

The Network folder appears.

A Each icon represents a computer on your local network.

4 Double-click the computer to which you want to connect.

OS X attempts to connect to the network computer. The attempt usually either fails or OS X logs on using the Guest account.

Note: The Guest account has only limited access to the network computer.

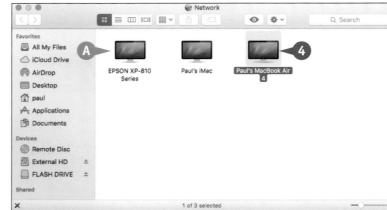

5 Click **Connect As**.

Your Mac prompts you to connect to the network computer.

6 Click the **Registered User** option (⭕ changes to ◉).

7 Type the username of an account on the network computer into the Name text box.

8 Type the password of the account into the Password text box.

9 To store the account data, click the **Remember this password in my keychain** check box (☐ changes to ☑).

10 Click **Connect**.

Ⓑ Your Mac connects to the computer and shows the shared resources that you can access.

11 When you are done, click **Disconnect**.

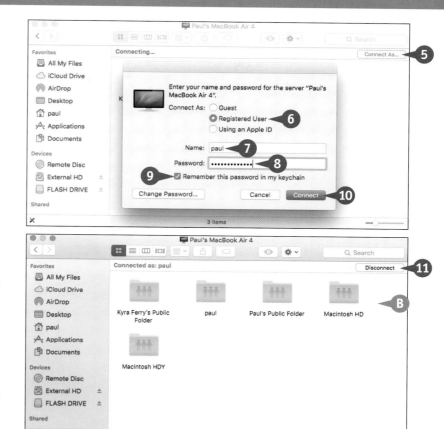

TIP

Is there a faster way to connect to a network computer?
Yes. In the Shared section of Finder's sidebar area, click the computer with which you want to connect (Ⓐ) and then follow steps **5** to **10** to connect as a registered user.

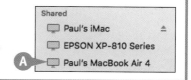

Turn On File and Printer Sharing

You can share your files with other network users. This enables those users to access your files over the network. Before you can share these resources, you must turn on your Mac's file-sharing feature. To learn how to share a particular folder, see the next section, "Share a Folder."

You can also share a printer that is connected directly to your Mac (such as via USB) with other network users. This enables those users to send print jobs to your printer over the network. Before this can happen, you must turn on your Mac's printer-sharing feature. To learn how to share a particular printer, see the section "Share a Printer," later in this chapter.

Turn On File and Printer Sharing

1 Click **Apple** ().

2 Click **System Preferences**.

The System Preferences window appears.

3 Click **Sharing**.

The Sharing preferences appear.

4 Click the **File Sharing** check box (☐ changes to ☑).

You can now share your folders, as described in the next section.

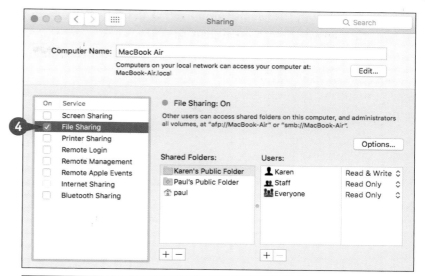

5 Click the **Printer Sharing** check box (☐ changes to ☑).

You can now share your printers, as described later in this chapter.

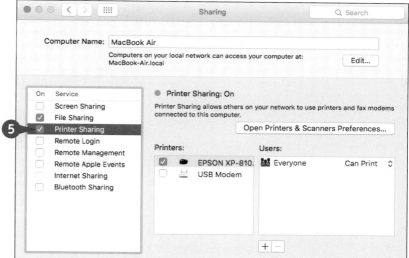

TIPS

How do I look up my Mac IP address?
In System Preferences, click ‹ to return to the main window and then click **Network**. Click **Wi-Fi** if you have a wireless network connection, or click **Ethernet** if you have a wired connection. In the Status section, read the IP address value.

What is the Public folder and how do I access it?
The Public folder is a special folder for sharing files. Anyone who connects to your Mac using your username and password has full access to the Public folder. To access the folder, click **Finder** (🙂), click **Go**, click **Home**, and then open the Public folder.

Share a Folder

You can share one of your folders on the network, enabling other network users to view and optionally edit the files you place in that folder. OS X automatically shares your user account's Public folder, but you can share other folders. Sharing a folder enables you to work on a file with other people without having to send them a copy of the file. OS X gives you complete control over how people access your shared folder. For example, you can allow users to make changes to the folder, or you can prevent changes.

Share a Folder

1 Open the Sharing preferences.

Note: See the previous section, "Turn On File and Printer Sharing," to learn how to display the Sharing preferences.

2 Click **File Sharing**.

Note: Be sure to click the **File Sharing** text, not the check box. This ensures that you do not accidentally uncheck the check box.

3 Under Shared Folders, click **Add** (+).

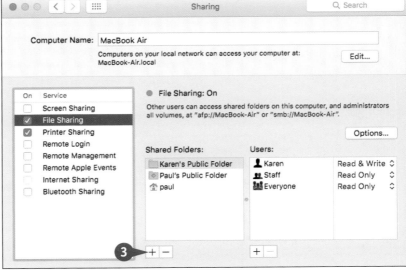

An Open dialog appears.

4 Click the folder you want to share.

5 Click **Add**.

Your Mac begins sharing the folder.

Note: You can also click and drag a folder from a Finder window and drop it on the list of shared folders.

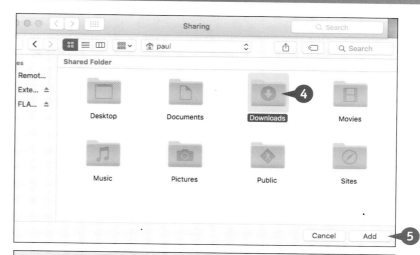

Ⓐ The folder appears in the Shared Folders list.

6 Click the folder.

7 For the Everyone user, click the current permission and then click the permission you want to assign.

Ⓑ The current permission is indicated with a check mark (✔).

OS X assigns the permission to the user.

Ⓒ You can also click **Add** (+) under the Users list to add more users.

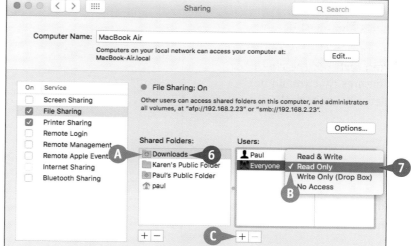

TIPS

What are the differences between the permission types?
Read & Write means users can open files, add new files, rename or delete existing files, and edit file contents. Read Only means users can only open and read files, but cannot make changes to files. Write Only (Drop Box) means users can add files to the folder as a Drop Box, but cannot open the folder. No Access means users cannot see the folder.

Can I share folders with Windows users?
Yes. In the Sharing window, click **Options** and then click **Share files and folders using SMB** (☐ changes to ☑). Click your user account (☐ changes to ☑), type your password, click **OK**, and then click **Done**.

Share a Printer

If you have a printer connected directly to your Mac, you can share the printer with the network. This enables other network users to send their documents to your printer, as long as your Mac is running. Sharing a printer saves you money because you only have to purchase one printer for all the computers on your network. Sharing a printer also saves you time because you only have to install, configure, and maintain a single printer for everyone on your network. See the next section, "Add a Shared Printer," to learn how to configure OS X to use a shared network printer.

Share a Printer

1 Click **Apple** (🍎).

2 Click **System Preferences**.

Note: You can also click **System Preferences** (⚙) in the Dock.

The System Preferences window appears.

3 Click **Sharing**.

④ Click **Printer Sharing**.

Note: Be sure to click the **Printer Sharing** text, not the check box. This ensures that you do not accidentally uncheck the check box.

⑤ Click the check box beside the printer you want to share (☐ changes to ☑).

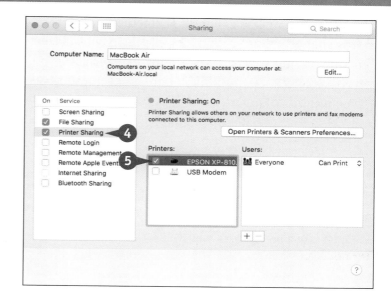

TIP

Is there another method I can use to share a printer?

Yes, you can follow these steps:

① Click **Apple** (🍎).

② Click **System Preferences**.

The System Preferences appear.

③ Click **Printers & Scanners**.

④ Click the printer you want to share.

⑤ Click the **Share this printer on the network** check box (☐ changes to ☑).

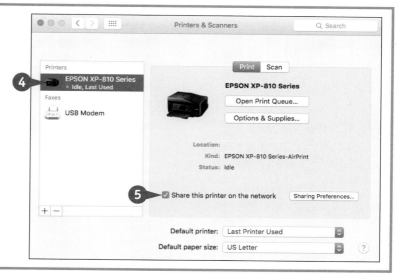

Add a Shared Printer

If another computer on your network has an attached printer that has been shared with the network, you can add that shared printer to your Mac. This enables you to send a document from your Mac to that shared printer, which means you can print your documents without having a printer attached directly to your Mac. Before you can print to a shared network printer, you must add the shared printer to OS X.

Add a Shared Printer

1 Click **System Preferences** (🔘) in the Dock.

The System Preferences window appears.

2 Click **Printers & Scanners**.

3 Click **Add** (+).

Note: If OS X displays a list of nearby printers, click the printer you want to add and skip the rest of these steps.

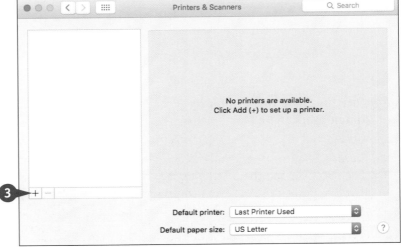

4 Click **Default**.

5 Click the shared printer.

A Look for the word *Bonjour* or the word *Shared* in the printer description.

6 Click **Add**.

Note: If OS X alerts you that it must install software for the printer, click **Download & Install**.

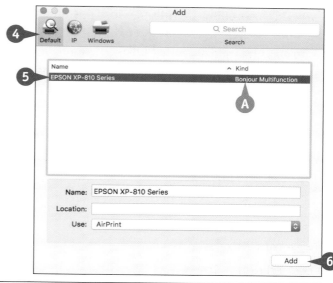

B OS X adds the printer.

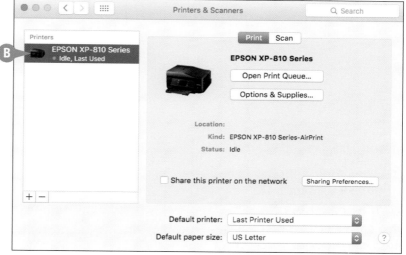

TIPS

Can I add a shared Windows printer?
Yes. Follow steps **1** to **3** and then click the **Windows** tab. Click the Windows workgroup, click the computer sharing the printer, log on to the computer, and then click the shared printer. In the Print Using list, click **Add** (+), click **Other**, and then click the printer in the list. Click **Add**.

How do I print to the shared printer that I added?
In any application that supports printing, click **File** and then click **Print**. In the Print dialog, click the **Printer** ⊙, click **Add** (+), and then click the shared printer. Choose your other printing options and then click **Print**.

View OS X on Your TV

If you have an Apple TV, you can use it to view your OS X screen on your TV. If you want to demonstrate something on your Mac to a group of people, it is difficult because most Mac screens are too small to see from a distance. However, if you have a TV or a projector nearby and you have an Apple TV device connected to that display, you can connect your Mac to the same wireless network and then send the OS X screen to the TV or projector. This is called AirPlay mirroring.

View OS X on Your TV

Mirror via System Preferences

1 Click **System Preferences** (⚙) in the Dock.

The System Preferences window appears.

2 Click **Displays**.

The display preferences appear.

3 Click the **AirPlay Display** ⬦ and then click your Apple TV.

OS X displays your Mac's screen on your TV.

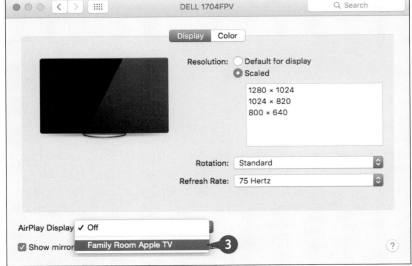

Mirror via the Menu Bar

1 Follow steps 1 and 2 to open the display preferences.

2 Click the **Show mirroring options in the menu bar when available** check box (☐ changes to ✓).

Ⓐ OS X adds the AirPlay Mirroring icon (📺) to the menu bar.

3 Click **Close** (●).

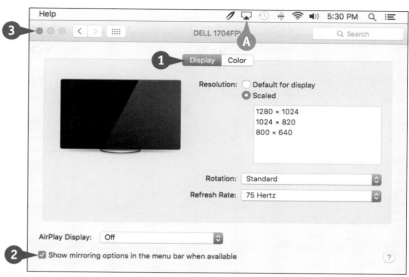

4 Click **AirPlay Mirroring** (📺).

5 Click your Apple TV.

OS X displays your Mac's screen on your TV (📺 changes to 📺).

TIPS

Is there an easy way to make my Mac's screen fit my TV screen?

Yes. If you have a high-resolution TV, the OS X screen might look small on the TV. Click **AirPlay Mirroring On** (📺) and then in the Match Desktop Size To section of the AirPlay Mirroring menu, click your Apple TV.

Can I use my TV as a second monitor for the OS X desktop?

Yes. This is useful if you need extra screen room to display the desktop and applications. Click **AirPlay Mirroring On** (📺) and then in the Use AirPlay Display To section of the AirPlay Mirroring menu, click **Extend Desktop**.

Index

S

Index